Imagine This

CREATING THE WORK YOU LOVE

Imagine This

CREATING THE WORK YOU LOVE

Maxine Clair

AUTHOR OF *RATTLEBONE* AND *OCTOBER SUITE*

BOLDEN

AN AGATE IMPRINT

CHICAGO

Library of Congress Cataloging-in-Publication Data

Clair, Maxine, 1939-
 Imagine this : creating the work you love / Maxine Clair.
    pages cm
  Includes bibliographical references.
  ISBN 978-1-932841-83-1 (paperback) -- ISBN 1-932841-83-0 (paperback) --
ISBN 978-1-57284-740-8 (ebook)
  1. Clair, Maxine, 1939---Philosophy. 2. Creative ability. 3. Expression (Philosophy)
4. Self-actualization (Psychology) 5. Conduct of life. 6. Clair, Maxine, 1939- 7.
African American women authors--Biography. 8. Women authors, American-
-Biography. I. Title.
  PS3553.L2225Z46 2014
  818'.5403--dc23
                          2014027146

Bolden is an imprint of Agate Publishing. Agate books are available in bulk at
discount prices. For more information visit agatepublishing.com

For Jackson, Noah, Nia, and Joseph
and always for Stephen, Michael, Joseph,
and Adrienne for this journey, this love

CONTENTS

INTRODUCTION

The sheer volume of writing about creativity suggests that the creative urge is always seeking an outlet and continually giving rise to the need for self-expression. Conscious creativity—the deliberate immersion in a talent, skill, or art—is a marker for some of the major transformational periods of our lives. For as long as humans have been here, we have advanced our understanding of who and what we are by putting forth such markers.

All over the world, in secret and in fame, people are either creating what they love, or looking to create it. At a young age, some of us chose a vehicle through which we could express, and claimed it as our talent. With guidance and exposure, we set out on a course, assured that it would bring us into grand ports of experience. In many cases, the creative expression that seemed to choose us at birth has delivered on the promise.

For dutiful others, soul searching has come through different channels. We have tried the meandering road to the skill or art encouraged by career counselors, aptitude statistics, or those who have taken our well-being to heart. Chances are, we made the commitment and it has proven worthwhile. Our self-expression may have fixed on a hobby or type of recreation—in a tool shed, in a kitchen, in a choir—that continues to contribute to a good life.

Occasionally, for some, there comes a moment that insists on deep introspection, and we come upon unspent energy: unused or underdeveloped capacities that push us toward what is at first a mystery. Like a vow of expansiveness, they win our attention. Engagement in conscious creative expression is a free-will choice to grow or to stand still.

The discovery of my own creative bent launched me on a journey inward, contemplating the questions of who I was and why I was here. In these pages, I have attempted to recount the journey so far. It has shed light on how creative expression can unify our inner and outer selves, consciously putting us in touch with the dual realities—human and spirit—in which we live and have our being. In many ways mine is the universal journey that dramatizes the mystery we all share—the mystery by which we were made manifest. It is no wonder that finding and developing that unique channel is both an imperative and a promise for anyone seeking to move beyond survival to living on purpose.

Yet for many it is not a conscious process. Being less than conscious can mean operating in the dark. A flourishing creative expression requires that we become conscious of being conscious. It requires that we clear the fog of limited thinking, doubt, and misperception.

If the creative impulse that you have always directed to the side entrance of your life is now knocking at the front door, or if you wish merely to feel the aliveness of expressing yourself and your search for the "how to" has not been fruitful, this book is for you. If you're at the point in life where the career that once afforded you contentment now seems narrow and thin, these pages point the way to choosing again. If the secret dream you've harbored for years is now infringing on all the traditions you've established, and if—for you—redirection is the new retirement, read on.

It doesn't matter whether you would love to own and operate a business, paint portraits, perform surgery or symphonies; whether you would love to spend your time and energy inventing or establishing something, immersing yourself in a cause, or learning finally what it means to live a sustainable life on the planet. Learn to consciously create the work that will bring you joy.

Ultimately, if and when we come to share our gift, we contribute to the evolution of the entire collective of humanity, and reap the sense of personal fulfillment. When we consciously claim the power to manifest that channel, we lay claim to being the co-creator, director, and star of our life.

The best way to make your dreams come true is to wake up.
—Paul Valery

1

WAKING UP

In the story of my happy childhood, every day is a tableau of summer: perpetual softball in the street, native scouts in the overgrown jungle near the cemetery, hide-and-go-seek with no out-of-bounds. On paydays, my father brings home a six-pack of Nehi soda pop that sates all our thirsts. At school I am a first-seat-first-row Cracker Jack, Miss Caruthers's helper, who makes S and S pluses on all my report cards. To while away time, my friends and I braid waves of buffalo grass on the side of the hill in the shade of the arched elms that line our street. Any given afternoon, I might fashion crepe paper into pinafores, weave plaited strips of fabric into extensions for my hair, and organize a talent show amid newspaper curtains thrown over the clothesline in the backyard. Our songs with made-up words entertain passersby on their way to Hy's Mar-

ket or Dairy Queen. At the piano, my mother—her perfect
hair dangling at her shoulders—can play anything anybody
can sing, so that when dusk falls, strains of some enchanting
melody drift out of the windows thrown open to let out the
day's heat.

In a montage of sweet memories, it is Sunday morning. Five
of the nine of us are already born and four are old enough to
get ourselves ready for church. We scurry around upstairs in
our two-story house. By now the bathwater comes out luke-
warm, and I am happy not to be the last in line. Downstairs
my mother scrapes the three-legged piano stool across the
hardwood floor. She spins the seat, lowering it to suit her. She
strikes up a chord or two, warming up. Then, with limber fingers, she romps through a few bars of "Jesus Is Real to Me" in
a hot gospel rhythm. By the time she abandons it, my brother
is coming as close as he can to singing the bass progressions.

Then, as I sit in the tub, she begins another song. It is a
melody that halts my hand's busy industry with the square
bar of Ivory inside a wad of faded terrycloth. I love this song,
not because its lyrics form the earliest rote of my Bible verses,
but because of the way it brings something akin to a quickening in my chest, and with it, the desire to fling my wet arms in
an arc above my head and, like a graceful ballerina, let them
open wide. My mother plays "The Lord Is My Shepherd." For
a self-conscious moment, I hold back, humming. I can hear
my brother somewhere between the kitchen and my parents'
bedroom, and I suppose that he is looking for the hairbrush.
He has already found his tenor line. My sister knows the
soprano line best. Another brother, young and eager, sings
in a wavery soprano; another, a baby voice, simply belts out
gibberish from the playpen downstairs. Then I, too, surrender
to the music. For as long as my mother will play it, we will
sing: my brother no doubt entranced between brush strokes,

my sister probably fiddling with her dress, the baby satisfied that she is one of us, and me perfectly still in the cool water.

In the story of my not-so-happy childhood, every day is marked by bleak winter. Poverty floats like a spirit that leaves a film on our windows when everyone else's windows are clear. It leaves clutter everywhere and becomes a thick something between floorboards that no amount of scrubbing can remove. All of us are born close, like stair-steps that follow each other, so that somebody else's dresses with safety-pinned waistlines and let-down hemlines become treasures. All of our dinners are boiled. I have no ribbons for ribbon day at school. In every grade, the same four people are smarter than I am, and all the girls have long hair. Miss Lightbody's voice is always saying that I talk too much, and Doretha Joley is always looking at my gray-white socks. Friends never enter our barrenness of little cheer and less substance. Even with prescribed headache powder, my headaches keep everyone up all night. My father works hard and long, paving sidewalks and building curbs. My mother plays heavy-burden church songs. Strains of their anger and strife penetrate the walls and drown out all possibilities of lightness.

In a composite of that view, here's a perfect moment: Poppa—my father's father—has died, and it is the morning of the funeral. My mother has brought her entire life to the piano. She sits on the piano stool, head thrown back, eyes closed, and sways her body with the rhythmic stroke of the keys as she sings, *Lord Jesus, can I have a talk with you?*

My mother is pregnant, and this day finds her with no maternity clothes suitable for a funeral. As I sit listening on the stairs, I see the paunch of her belly beneath the pale green chenille robe. Doing things the way she and my father do things, he has gone—at the last minute—to buy her a dress.

I am old enough to know that his choice ultimately will be governed by the dollars we don't have. I am old enough to know, too, that the emotion in my mother's plaintive song is not wholly due to Poppa's death. The perpetual sorrow that bleeds out through the slow syncopation of minor chords, the crescendo of pain in her voice as she sings—I read it all as a lament about the emotional and material poverty of her life. And I have come to expect that at any moment she will go quiet in a wash of tears. I am her oldest daughter; I would do anything to save her from that.

As those stories took form, I believed that behind the scenes, God was the power that made things happen. Like a sustained musical drone that holds the entire piece together, God Almighty remained on the throne deciding who gets what and why. He was an easy, reward-or-punishment God. We were Christians. My mother played piano for our church, my father sang in the choir, we seldom missed Sunday School or Baptist Training Union. Everything about my life was clearly tied to religion, the moral compass by which our family was supposed to live.

Both the blessing and the curse is that eventually some aspects of childhood come to an end. What we consciously choose as our creative means of expression in the world—and how—can be instructive. When we "put away childish things," we sometimes abandon the sense of wonder and adventure we once knew as play. And we sometimes make obstacles of the not-so-great memories, and spend our lives striving to overcome them. These stories can go on, framing what we believe about who we are, what we should be doing, and how the world works. Unwittingly for the most part, we create a life within that mindset—or we can shape-shift the frame, or even allow the old frame to fall away completely.

Life is always intervening on our behalf, alerting us to the fact that the way we are framing life is or is not working, and we're at a point where we can choose to see differently. When we don't hear the alarm, life seems to turn up the volume.

One listless day in the summer of my 14th year, an event took up residence in my psyche the way an invisible entity might insinuate itself into the woodwork of the room where I slept.

Typical of Kansas and the Great Plains in general, the sky that day was an endless, stark blue. Against such a backdrop, anything—a cumulus cloud, a vapor trail, a hawk gliding on the wind—suggested drama. My brother and I stood in our front yard watching two fighter jets as they circled overhead, going in for a landing at Fairfax Field a few miles away. Pilots in training, showing off their corkscrew dives, were not an unusual sight. But a few minutes later, they came around again, flying parallel. Then one of them broke formation, flying lower. Suddenly it was directly overhead with a powerful roar and the intimacy of all that steel; we could see dark seams of wheel wells and rivets like a pox along the belly.

"He's flying too low!" my brother yelled.

We watched the plane going down in a long whine beyond trees and houses a neighborhood away. The ground quivered. One explosion after another sent up fireballs and black smoke. Neighbors stood on their porches hugging their elbows in bewilderment.

I felt shaken, yet drawn to the horror. Our mother warned us, "Stay here."

Into the next day, we heard news of second stories being sheared off houses. As time passed and we were allowed to go near the devastation, I took in the tally of deaths, which included one of our local high-school teachers, the pilot, and workers in the car lot where the plane finally burned to a hulk.

I had no language for trauma then. Probably I relied on the hope that God's only son, Jesus, was perpetually interceding on our behalf. Probably I reflected on the crash as a rational fact of mechanical failure, swallowed up in the inscrutable will—synonymous with "wrath"—of God.

I don't remember exactly when they began, but for the next 20 years, recurring dreams of the crash plagued my sleep. Throughout my teens, I would have a spate of them over short periods. Then, with no predictable trigger or pattern, years would pass before I would have another.

By grace and whatever menial jobs I could find, I went to college, where, true to my aptitude, I aimed for and achieved a science degree. Away from home, the nightmares lingered—me and my brother in the yard, the roar of the planes, the premonition of disaster, the fire and clamor that implied many deaths. I would startle awake in my dorm, wondering if my family at home was all right.

It was in college that I turned away from my Baptist upbringing. Picture the cavernous sanctuary of a Catholic church, the sacristy, the altar draped in crisp white with gold piping. Picture stained-glass windows where streaming sunlight illuminates the iconic stations of the cross. Picture a golden chalice raised high in the hands of an august priest whose flowing robes signify reverence. The first time I touched my fingers into the small vessel of tepid holy water I knew that this ceremonial grandeur was for me. I looked to it for a deeper experience of the sacred. Decades into the future, the allure of ritual would fade, and I would confess my disbelief and resistance to the catechism.

In the intervening years, however, I was completely absorbed by marriage, and the awesome process of raising a family. After the first two children, we began climbing our comparable career ladders in earnest, with all the attendant ups and downs. I was a medical technologist at a university hospital. He taught high school. Like a rash that breaks out every now and then, the crash nightmare was something I lived with, just as I was learning to live with a secret, seething discord.

The first irrefutable proof of our plunge into the pit from which there would be no return came one afternoon when my husband and I were standing in the tiny bathroom of our rental house. I can still see the black-and-white tile of the floor and the ancient bathtub with its clubfeet. We were having a heated argument about something that must have been important.

At some point, I said something caustic, and he came back with something mean. I said something dismissive and hostility saturated the bathroom.

When he slapped me, it was as if lightning had struck too hot and quick for my mind to catch up. I was more shocked than hurt; I had never been slapped before. By the time reason filtered in, he was gone, only to return later, not appropriately full of remorse, not even very apologetic. I was at a loss. The cliché of a bottom line was that I loved him in all the ways I knew love to be. I believed that he needed me to show him that I loved him, and I was not always able to intuit what that meant. I believed that he loved me, too. I saw him as someone with a "hot temper," and some men could be like that. When he apologized, saying how upset I had made him, I forgave him his faults.

When it comes to culpability, self-doubt is as much a vortex for blame as blame is for guilt, and as guilt is for one's sense of worth. I tried to understand what I was doing wrong. I did not hear the "mind-frame" alarm from the universe.

For a while we got along okay. He got into law school; we moved to the East Coast.

By the time we had our third son and first daughter a year apart, I had collected a silent litany of complaints about the difficulty of keeping a family together. But after law school, I thought I could see daylight. We would begin anew.

Fast-forward through years of work, childcare, and homework; of dodging Catholic Mass, with me praying nonetheless; of making ends meet and trudging through a hush-hush mayhem. Throughout those struggles, there came the second time, then a third and a tenth time, when one crisis or another, one bad day or another, one minor or major disagreement, provoked him into a violent fit and I bore the brunt of his rage. Any halfway alert intelligence would have noticed my personality losing altitude, but I was in denial about what constituted the ultimate deal-breaker. I was caught in the fierce combination of thinking that I needed to make it work and being plain-and-simple scared.

During those years I experienced the crash scenario more as a dream than a nightmare: I am standing alone in the front yard of my childhood home in Kansas. I happen to glance up into a clear blue sky, and catch the dazzling glint of a high-flying silver plane—just one—so high that it looks like a toy. There is no noise. As I stand watching, the plane makes loops in the air and small but graceful up-and-down motions, like a seal humping water.

In the way of dreams, I know that though the plane appears to be having a successful exercise, in reality it is out of control. I know, too, that the pilot is unaware of this fact. I realize that it is up to me to somehow communicate to him that he is in trouble. I jump up and down in the yard, waving my arms, desperate to get his attention. Helplessly, I watch as the plane begins to fall sideways, slow and silent as death. It falls just beyond the familiar trees and houses in the distance. When the explosions and conflagration ensue,

I know that I have failed to save him and all the others. Always, I awake disconsolate.

In my catalogue of discontent, religion loomed large, second only to marriage woes. Love and fear were no longer opposites. Separated down here from a God up there, who wielded bolts of approval or reproach depending on whether or not He was well pleased, I switched allegiances again, this time to the ethical foundations of the Unitarian philosophy. Still, in the turmoil of my home life, old beliefs held sway.

People look for physical signs—bruises, scars—in order to judge the scope of violation; just how bad was it? You can count scars and bruises all day and never get at the real damage. The body knows how to heal itself. Healing mind and spirit, however, requires a different magnitude of care. Even if you've read the manual, you learn by right of consciousness. That is to say, the level of awareness with which you conduct your everyday life determines the insight into how you will heal your spirit. I was a woman who believed, unwittingly, that her worth and value depended on her ability to fix, humanize, rescue, or otherwise save a "loved one," and so the victim role was tailor-made for me. How does one hear the alarm and shape-shift the mind-frame?

First you would have to learn to get over your sense of shame for having a Saturday-night-brawl kind of marriage. You would have to stop caring that anyone knows, or that the vague "they" gossip about the details. You would have to get a grip on what it means to keep your mouth shut, and not object to either his subtle or blatant ways of putting you in your place. You would have to have enough of whatever it takes not to pretend that you're coping, and you would have to worry more about the obscenity of it all than about finding room in your heart for tolerance. You would have to spend your money on counseling instead of buying the right kind of makeup to conceal the signs, which would mean, too, that you have been concealing the part of yourself that wants out. You would have to start noticing that you've learned to lie equally convincingly about important and inconsequential things, consenting to what you abhor, colluding in the case against yourself. You would have to face the fact that every time you have nodded your head yes when your heart was screaming no, you have lost another chit of self-respect. If you don't hear the alarm, you end up trying to build a life based on your mistaken belief about a valuable self.

By the umpteenth punch or laceration or bruise, though, you see that fear has become the atmosphere in which you exist. You resort to daydreaming of ways to disappear with the children. Each time your mind entertains another wild escape, you come back to the reality of square one to find that you have forfeited too many degrees of courage.

Somewhere along that timeline, you pore over a news article about a local woman who had died "by accident" when her local-official husband shoved her backward and stormed out of the house, performed his official duties all day, and returned that evening to find that the concussion she suffered when she struck her head against the bedside table had proved fatal. Life is turning up the volume.

There is nothing that can focus the mind and its intentions like an immediate threat to survival. Then comes the night that you're lying on a gurney in the emergency room with a fracture and stitches. Dignity, fear, and your overdeveloped sense of responsibility for saving the world—all are clearly irrelevant. You catch the faintest hint of the basic truth that your worth depends on rescuing no one but yourself. It becomes an absolute certainty that if you are to die by his hand, you will die mid-stride as you walk away.

In the macrocosmic wake of social change it was easy to shape the microcosmic narrative of that time of my life into a heroic one. This woman who had once colluded in the perception of powerlessness became an empowered woman, no longer willing to buy into a warped notion of love. The fact is, you cannot be swept up by any movement unless you are ready for change. Although my husband had unshakeable ideas about unbreakable unions, there was no turning back for me, and without the slightest tremor, I sought divorce.

One morning, I awoke alone in my bed, house quiet, children still asleep. I was 34. My oldest son was 12, my baby girl was 4. Despite all the threats and our dire financial circumstances, I had won the separation agreement that would eventually lead to divorce. As I came awake that morning, I was aware of a stillness unlike any I had ever experienced. Once I was fully awake, I recalled this lucid dream: I am standing alone in the front yard of my family's house in Kansas. I see a tiny plane, silver, reflecting the sun. I see it make its loops, hump the air. And I say to my dreaming self, *I am dreaming this crash dream again.*

With that, the tiny plane suddenly halts high in the air, and begins to fly in reverse. Noiselessly, level and balanced, it backs up across the sky. Ever so carefully, it glides backwards, down an invisible mountain of air. As it gets closer, it grows bigger. It continues its reverse flight—this big, silent, silver bird—drifting right past me to land, tail-end-first, gently in the middle of my street. And I say to my dreaming self, *I will never have this dream again.*

After 20 years the recurring dream was finished. That morning I understood many things. I had received the message of *no crash, safe landing*, and I knew with certainty that I would be all right. I had finally connected with the pilot of that dream plane. Clear and simple, I had connected with something—a guidance, an assurance—that was greater than I knew myself to be.

My powerlessness was over. This watershed of awareness—greater self-awareness, and awareness of a greater self—marked the end of living in a dream and the beginning of waking up. I was poised to find a way to stand up in the world.

~

What wakes us up? The workings of our own physiology reveal a certain kind of movement: circadian rhythms, the "biological clock," determine our sleeping and waking patterns. Just by virtue of being born on this planet, and crucial to survival here, regardless of conditions of light or darkness, sound, silence or activity—these rhythms hold sway. The sun sets and we wind down toward sleep. At dawn, deep sleep gives way to more shallow levels until the senses break into consciousness. As if to open a deeper space within, we stretch and yawn, move slowly, regain some vigor, and finally we're physically awake.

In the psychological and spiritual realm, we could say that waking up occurs by a cosmic rhythm. Some inseparable something within us allows unawareness only for so long, and then awareness dawns. As a fundamental requirement for the evolution of consciousness, we become aware of new and different aspects of what we know as reality.

Waking up sometimes occurs in infinitesimally small steps, over years, and sometimes in quantum leaps; sometimes with drama, often with subtlety. Just as our biological cycles are spelled out by age and physiology—puberty, adolescence, adulthood—awakenings, too, have their rhythm. Something within expands, allowing more expression of our human and spiritual nature. In an unknowable gestation cycle, we come into a time of shedding the old and discovering a new way of being in the world. Perhaps as we go through life, we are always in one stage or another of expansion: the little life we're in cannot contain all the living within us, and life gets bigger.

Whether an extended process or a moment of sudden illumination, and whether or not we choose to open to it, inborn in us is the possibility of being more deeply aware.

Again and again we get glimpses or full panoramas that show us the truth of our wisdom or ignorance, the visionary or blind choices we have made. We become conscious of the possibility of release from how we have been living in the world, and move with vigor to more expanded ways.

Seeking that deeper wakefulness is a natural impulse. No matter where we are in life, some part of us is always looking for the clarity that self-awareness can bring, and for the peace and joy that is the promise of spiritual transformation. Yet we sometimes imagine that we don't have what it takes to pursue those ends. Our busy lives, our confusion of ideas, our multitasking to keep up with exploding innovations on the planet—all of this can make it feel like we simply don't have the time or the focus to develop the habits of reflection.

Perhaps this is why crises render us so amenable to waking up. There is no question that an urgent dilemma sharpens our focus. For better or worse, things we once relied on no longer serve us, and we may be more willing to risk exploration of unknown territories. The question *Why did this happen to me?* presses us to examine what we believe about cause and effect, and possibly to consider things to which we have never given serious thought.

When we become masters of accommodating our fears and longings, we deaden our sensitivity to true awareness. Crises are situations where we are challenged to choose either to be open to new answers, or to burrow more deeply into the darkness of our own despair. In his book *Power vs. Force: The Hidden Determinants of Human Behavior*, David Hawkins proposes, "On our scale of consciousness, there are two critical points that allow for major advancement: the first is at... the initial level of empowerment. Here the willingness to stop blaming and accept responsibility for our own actions, feelings, [and] beliefs arises—as long as cause and responsibility are projected outside of oneself, one will remain in the powerless mode of victimhood."

It is always a choice. We can remain asleep in a consciousness that supports the belief that life happens to us. Usually there is no reason to doubt it: we can prove it to ourselves, and our selves will believe it. And often, too, we follow an arbitrary opinion poll about what is right and wrong, what we must do, and who we ought to be. Subscribing to the blame game keeps us static, pinpointing the shortcomings of innumerable others who got in our way. With honesty we can list the uncaring powers in society that hold us back. This is the norm, and it can be counterproductive, preventing other forces affecting our lives from appearing on our personal radars.

Or we can wake up. Pay attention. Notice life. Look at our personal responses to what seems to occur, and make note of the endless patterns we've established. It's an inside job. The shifts we experience—toward freedom, peace, and clarity—are invaluable gifts.

Cultivating the Practice of Sacred Journaling

How do we come to more wakefulness? If you were not aware of your own awakenings, you probably would not be reading this book. If, however, you feel called to the idea of exploring them, or inviting greater wakefulness, I can share my own experience with establishing new habits.

Sacred practices—sacred because they concerned my relationship with myself and with all that is—were vital to me in coming into a better life. Meditation, affirmation, journaling, giving without attachment, clearing my mind are but a few. Your work is the time and energy you devote to the practices.

In pursuing a greater sense of wakefulness and alertness to life, you necessarily give more attention to the things you control: what you think, what you say and do, your attitudes and beliefs. Give yourself permission to try any practices that you find anywhere—including here—and take whatever you find useful as your own. You can teach your body to be in accord with what occurs when you are situated in the appropriate, chosen time and place. You can equip yourself with all that you need to establish the new practices—a comfortable environment, materials, and implements.

During that exhilarating period of my new freedom, one of the first habits I acquired was that of writing down my self-talk. It turned out to be one of the most productive processes I have ever undertaken. Among other things, journaling became my gateway to the sacred practice of deliberate meditation and other life-affirming processes.

This sacred journaling is not to be confused with conventional diary-keeping in which you chronicle the day-to-day details of your life. You are not so much keeping a record of your life's events and activities as bringing into conscious focus the millions of similar and dissimilar things that wander through your mind and experience: events, revelations, ideas, synchronicities, intuitions, reflections, secrets, memories, beliefs, the mystical—anything and everything that fits into the general category of an inner life.

This "writing it down" slows the speed at which things first occur to you, things that all too quickly fly in the wind of forgetfulness. This gives you time to focus, which is to say, you allow them to register.

High on the list of reasons to journal is the opportunity to examine your own mind: to become more familiar with what you think, how you think, what you believe, your reactions, and how you respond to experience based on what seems to occur. In other words, it gets you to the "why" of your actions.

Journaling creates the opportunity to revisit and mine your inner workings for the treasure they hold. As you write, you talk to yourself about whatever arises, and your responses to it. You process what occurs to you and what you make of what occurs to you; you record ideas that leap out, and where they might lead.

Periodically, as you become a reader of your journal, you take the vantage point of an observer with a more objective point of view. What if, in all that material, the connections were clear and relevant? The observer's role can reveal to you attitudes and beliefs that may be based on the hidden assumptions you've been holding, the feelings and thoughts that limit your experience. No longer are you caught up in the experience that you attempted to record accurately. By journaling, you build the habit of expectation outside of the "normal" way things seem to unfold. Revelations gel into new views of how things work; dreams deliver clues about waking life; synchronicities suggest a new framework for interpretation and expansion.

You begin to see this kind of clarifying as a part of the bigger process that involves you and the cosmos, a concrete way to contemplate and reflect. Your creativity, your awareness, and your personal and spiritual growth are all served by this. You'll find that daily, sometimes even as you come awake, you get an out-of-nowhere, light-bulb idea. The stream may pour forth as a continuation of an idea you had yesterday or last year. Sometimes it is absolute clarity about the truth of who you are. Although it may involve issues and challenges, the powerful impulse to sort out a message or an interpretation will take root.

The challenge is that the mind that writes is the same mind that gets its sense of self from experience. And so, if your not-so-happy childhood story is one of, say, abandonment, if you have been creating a life based on the perception that that is what friends need to know about who you are, if you have derived your sense of self from being left behind, it can be challenging to examine your self-talk from a perspective of someone who was cherished. Still, the process is worth the time and effort. If it turns out that you need to seek the assistance of a professional to sort out the details, in the name of love, give yourself permission to do that.

And so "writing it down"—for better or for worse—is a way to chronicle the evolution of your journey of discovery as you dance around the perennial mystery of who you are and why you are here and where you are going.

Your story goes on. If establishing a different slant on the past becomes the new story, that version, too, is probably temporary in the unfolding of your life. When you hit on an essential truth, you will know that it undercuts every story you may have told yourself.

If you find dream-journaling to be productive, use it. Amateur and scholarly books on dream interpretation abound, and you will have no trouble finding one that speaks to you. A rule of thumb for my personal explorations of dreams is that, for the most part, the details in dreams—whether symbolic, metaphoric, or concrete, and no matter the cast of characters—have always been about me, my life, my relationship with myself, and my relationship with everything and everyone else.

One more thing: don't underestimate the importance of aesthetics. Choose the journal that is yours—you'll know it when you see it. Shop online and feast on all the lovely choices. You may want to consider something in hardback that can accommodate a considerable volume of daily entries. To encourage the flow you wish to establish as you write, choose something larger than five by seven inches, with lined or unlined pages, and with no markings or images to distract you.

Journaling Exercises

1. Recall a time when you had a "waking up" experience: an insight that brought new awareness, major or small. How did it change you or your life? Starting with what you recall about that moment or period, begin journal-keeping today.

Each day, record and describe any serendipities—the events that seem to be fortunate discoveries and seem to be by chance. Record synchronicities—the meaningfully related "coincidences" in time that have no obvious related cause. Keep track of any insights you have, whether or not they seem significant. Journal anything else that interests you about this time in your life.

Keep your journal handy. You will be surprised by the inner processing that occurs in the car or on the metro. If you find it more suitable to divide entries by category—gratitude, dreams, insights, intentions, etc.—do not hesitate to section off the pages. Remember that this is a personal journal, not to be shared indiscriminately. Perceptions change. Beliefs evolve. Ideas develop into things you have yet to imagine. What you wrote yesterday may contradict what you will write tomorrow, and so be it. We are all "in process."

2. In your journal, make a list of possibilities, then decide on at least one activity daily that gives you the sense that you are caring for your mental, physical, and spiritual well-being. For example:

- For body-mind emphasis, treat yourself to a massage, or a session with one of various therapeutic energy practitioners.
- Read an uplifting book or article in a magazine that is new to you. Check online or at your favorite newsstand or bookstore for titles in spiritual living, fitness, philosophical ideas, literary masterpieces—whatever interests you.
- Spend some solitude in your favorite natural environment. Go to places—actual and imaginary—where you feel closest to your higher being-ness.

3. Institute a media fast for a week, and notice the level of mind chatter you entertain, and the silences in between.

4. Begin to notice and jot down the ways that people all around you are expressing their particular gifts. Consider which gifts you are expressing.

Creativity can be described as letting go of certainties.
—Gail Sheehy

2
HOVERING BETWEEN ENDINGS AND BEGINNINGS

I n the film version of survival or "waking up" stories, the very next frame shows the woman putting on the armor of self-respect, taking on the world in a self-sufficient way, and viewing vistas that suggest living happily ever after. As the credits roll, you see cascading images of a boardroom, standing ovations, awards, and the second-time-around wedding. Don't fail to miss the point: that in actual life, it's not about an implausible carefree existence that lasts into a magical ever-after. Instead, it's about *living*, as opposed to merely existing or making do, ever after.

Waking up, coming into greater awareness, is a transformative shift, and the newness of it can be exhilarating. The prospect of a new interior can transport you to simply being with what is, and seeing the new plateau as a blessed resting place. At such a comfortable juncture, you may do as I did and begin to reflect about what, indeed, you are aware of. For one thing, perhaps you've come to know that you own yourself, your life. You can choose, and without choice, there is no real freedom. Or, if you've always known this, you become aware of the joy of simply being alive, which can inform all your days. And with that comes a deeper sense of gratitude.

I can remember feeling thankful for everything and no particular thing. There were many mornings when I awoke more aware of so much that I had taken for granted: trees shouting in blossoms or exploding in shades of autumn's hallelujah; snow quietly softening the contours of the visible and invisible world; a bird's concerto never failing to pierce the heart; a good meal bringing comfort beyond the body. Awareness of what? Maybe you are grateful merely that the sun has risen, and your body walks upon the earth. You find that the deeper gratitude into which you have come is a natural response to being alive. And don't you want to share it? To share, too, is a naturally occurring aspect of awakening.

At the top of my list when my ship sailed was to do something singularly spectacular for my mother. Abandoned by one parent, then pregnant at 15, she submitted to an arrangement by her mother and my father's father that turned out to be a shotgun wedding. She took on marriage as a life sentence of guilt and shame. I believed that, at a time when something better was still possible, she must have been filled with the promise of mornings. But like so many women of her generation, she never escaped the stream of a cup always poured out dutifully by one lord of her life or another, and always half empty. I believed that regret and resentment ripened and dried up to bitter pills difficult to swallow and always under-cutting her sense of worth.

Here I was, a young woman testing the waters of change and hope, while she remained a locked-out, unhappy victim of life. For so many years I had seen myself as her go-to person, her confidant, the holder of her secrets and confessor of her resentments, her personal resource for books and tapes. She was coming up on 60 years old, and someday she would leave the earth. I was determined that that should not happen before she had lived—and no one had lived who had never seen an ocean.

A family vacation was the answer: a far-away-but-drive-to place; siblings and their families in separate houses close by; broken routines, endless sun, and water. Big water. For me, the engine that drove this whole enterprise was my desire that, for the first time in her life, my mother should see the ocean.

Jekyll, one of Georgia's Sea Islands, was the spot. We made plans. Summer arrived. I drove south with my children. From landlocked Kansas, a family caravan made its meandering way to the coast. We arrived one night under a gibbous moon that had already climbed half the sky. The backyard patio of my parents' rental opened onto a path that led to the waves just beyond the dunes. What a moment for my mother to see the ocean for the first time.

"Not tonight. It'll still be there in the morning," my mother said. I knew that they were all tired, but I knew, too, that they did not understand what they were missing.

I urged, "But you've got to see it on a night like this with the moon so bright it's like sunlight on the water."

"There'll be other nights." My mother smiled as if she were amused at my impatience. And I thought, *That's all*

*right. I have waited all this time to share it, and she has waited
a lifetime without knowing about the line she will soon cross.
Tomorrow then.*

The next morning, my children, my sisters, and I hit the
floor at dawn to get a jump on sunrise and waves. We jogged
down the beach to my parents' house. No one stirred there. If
you've ever listened to the sheer sonic novelty of waves crashing, you couldn't help but be dumbfounded that my mother
couldn't respond to an ocean in her backyard.

We made a pretense of casually waiting on their patio. By
the time she appeared, delighted squeals of the family were
competing with the pounding surf.

"Come on," I coaxed. "You've *got* to see this."

She said, "Okay, I'm coming."

She was wearing a very modest navy-blue swimsuit, a
flared cut that amply covered her full figure, with a crisp
white V at the neckline. I watched as, arm-in-arm, she and
my grandmother made their way slowly. Warm sand oozed
around their flip-flops.

Across the dunes they came, my mother now walking
alone, a little ahead of my grandmother. I held my breath for
what was coming. When she got to where the beach sloped
away, she stopped. The sand was wet and firm. Exhausted
waves washed up and soaked in, forcing tiny burps of air to
the surface. My mother looked up the beach toward the bend,
then down the beach toward the low-lying convention center,
surveying the situation.

From farther into the breakers, I made my grand, sweeping gesture and yelled, "The ocean!" I couldn't wait to know
what she was thinking.

She fanned her hand in dismissal and yelled something
that was lost in the flat air, and when I cocked my ear, she

said something about needing beach chairs to sit on, "…so we don't get all full of sand."

My thought had been simply for her first to take in the splendor, and to bother with chairs and umbrellas later.

She shaded her eyes with her hands, looked out across the water, and said something like, "Yeah, it's very nice. Nice breeze right here, too." My sisters lugged all the beach paraphernalia and they sat down.

Crestfallen, I splashed with the kids, baptized myself and waded out beyond the breakers. In the warm current, I practiced my sidestroke, swimming along the shoreline where my mother could see me. I treaded water and waved to her and my grandmother, sitting side by side near the dunes.

Despite the fact that my mother was unimpressed by the ocean, the first day was truly terrific. The second day, though, I was determined that my mother should at least get her feet wet. Wet feet were all I would ask.

And so that next day we walked, my mother and I, up the beach. I moved on a diagonal toward the water. She held to her straight line. I reached for her hand.

"Walk with me just to the edge where you can get your feet wet." I pointed to the kids, knee deep in the surf. "They like it. We won't even go that far out."

She shook her head. "Um-um, no."

In awe, there is always the possibility of dread. This time I was close enough to see that she was frightened. This stroll along the Atlantic's crashing waves now seemed more than I should have hoped for.

I didn't know it then, but in the midst of one of life's transformative moments, it can be next to impossible to let life be however it is. You can come up against the reality of a shifting relationship with those you love. Comfortable bonds can reconfigure themselves in ways that tamper with your heart connection. I could not give my mother the sense of wonder and exhilaration I wanted her to have. Nobody could.

"It's too much," my mother said, wagging her head, but smiling.

"I know," I told her, "I know."

Before the week ended, my mother spent a good part of several days sitting in the sand short of the breakers, letting spent waves wash over her legs and feet.

Fixed somewhere between memory and imagination is this image: my mother stands on the shore, shading her eyes against the sun, and I am in the water, pushing off.

Whenever you're poised between a known past and an unknown future, you have the opportunity to reflect on the bridge where you stand. Depending upon the day of the week, or the hour of the day, you may find yourself heavy with the weight of endings, the joy and grief they bring, the empty spaces they leave.

Endings are the first stage of new beginnings, and they are precipitated by the dynamism of life. They come with the fact of evolution: in this life, nothing stays the same. In the preface to the second edition of his book *Transitions*, William C. Bridges writes, "Without a transition [transformation], change is just a rearrangement of the furniture." When you are undergoing transformation, you are drafting the blueprint of a new house where the old furniture cannot fit.

Endings are not always wrapped and tied neatly. They can be a mess of bewildering details with the worst possible timing. They can occur with a randomness that makes no rational sense. Sudden, devastating events can precipitate radical transformation: climate events and geological changes come to mind.

Loss—of loved ones, possessions, status, relationships, health—also presents a major turning point. Loss brings on grief, and emotional turmoil is inevitable. In such a vulnerable state, we may discover that everything is slowing down, and we settle in to simply being with what is—the surges and crashes of emotional distress, the physical symptoms, the questioning of spiritual belief. These are necessary parts of the grieving process.

With any loss, it is not uncommon to fall into the mode of perception that defines life mainly as what happens *to* us. At times like these, deeper understanding may not be a priority. We may not yet be able to accept the boundaries of birth and death that come with the human condition. We may not yet be ready to look at life as being also what we think, say, and do: the beliefs and attitudes that can manifest as failed relationships or unwise career moves. Introspection about our response to a loss may come after our survival is assured. It is important to give ourselves permission to be where we are in the unfolding of these circumstances, and give ourselves the utmost gentle care. We may find that love and support are available in unpredictable ways. Becoming aware of where we are in this process is key to sensing when—days, months, years—we are open to adjusting to life without the thing we so valued. The process is ongoing as we begin to move on.

The end of things as they have been can inform our life for a short period or stretch out for decades. When we come to accept that something or someone is gone from our life, or accept that we must let go of what no longer serves us— whether or not we are happy with the release—there is more space for living anew. As challenging as it may be, letting go of a particular part of a past identity can release us from rigid, albeit familiar, roles.

Cultivating the Practice of Affirming Life

Nobody enjoys living in fear, worry, and doubt. Nobody prefers poverty over abundance or discord over harmony. We all want to feel whole. Yet we often respond to our ever-changing experiences of life from the mind-frames that come with gloomy stories we tell ourselves, the stories we believe our lives to be. Our expectations sometimes arise from the perception that in endings, there is always something wrong: that life is punishing us, or something bad is on the horizon. Life is against us and we must defend against it. We can make a mind-enemy of a flower, a job opportunity, or time of day just as easily as we make a mind-enemy of a co-worker. We fight life by feeling, thinking, seeing, and believing from an automatically negative mind-frame—automatic because we are totally unaware that it exists within us.

How do we change that? I offer no absolutes, but in Chapter 5 you will find more details about clearing your mind. For now, consider that you can create statements that will foster positive beliefs and attitudes. In doing so, you train your patterns of thinking and manifest new, desirable experience.

Conscious or unconscious, and whether they are thought or spoken aloud, you continually use affirmations, assertions of the belief that something is true. The principle involved is simple: whatever you focus on or whatever you hold in your mind will expand in your experience.

You may have heard this metaphysical proposition referred to as the law of attraction, law of manifestation, self-fulfilling prophesy, and other terms. It is rooted in the assumption of an ultimate reality in which thoughts and beliefs are *things*, and they have a powerful role in manifesting experience. By working with affirmations, you begin the process of replacing unsound beliefs, unproductive habits, misguided perceptions, and flawed thinking that may be limiting your experience of the life you want. You replace them with life-affirming thought and belief. With regular practice, you can be more deeply in touch with your authentic self, which is foundational to desirable experience.

There are logical elements which make up the prescribed formulation of an affirmation. First, it should be stated in the **present tense**, as if it is already true. For example, *I am alert, open, and receptive to all my good.* When you state an affirmation in present tense, you are holding in mind the completed thing you want to do, be, or have— not the hope of it. If you state it as a future hope—*I am going to have the perfect career doing what I want*—the results will always be waiting to happen. If you focus on the "how to," you limit the greatest possible outcome.

Use **positive** statements. Affirm what you do want rather than what you do not want. *I don't want to fail* is a negative statement. Rather affirm, *For the highest good, I now enjoy complete success.* The positive statement reinforces your intention.

Make your statement **personal** and **precise**. Keeping it specific and brief adds power. Affirmations that roll off your tongue have a greater impact at a subconscious level than those that are stilted. The more "right" the affirmation feels to you, the deeper the impression it makes on your mind, and the sooner you will experience the desired outcome. So use your own language, make the idea as clear and uncluttered as possible, and fine-tune it over time.

There will be more later about ultimate power, but for affirmations, your power comes from your belief. The conviction you *feel* is the power that drives the process. Initially you may not fully believe your affirmation, but belief will come. Sense of certainty arises as you persist. And persistence requires repetition—you repeat and repeat the affirmation to train the mind.

Remember that, in all likelihood, with an affirmation you are replacing a limiting belief of which you are not aware. Focus on only what you want to manifest. Whatever you believe, whatever you can visualize or imagine, whatever you can accept, expands in your experience.

Bridge affirmations provide another avenue from disbelief to belief. When you simply cannot find the actual words because some part of you cannot accept the possibility of what you wish or hope to do, be or have, an affirmation about belief or clarity can serve. For example: *For the highest good, I am open to deeper belief in my dream.* That's taking it one step at a time.

For all your affirmation work, act *as if*. Remember repetition is the key to staying on track, and that includes your actions. When you ask yourself, "What do I really want?," write down the answers and establish your statements around them. Review your statements for as long as it takes to have the language, clarity, and detail you want. Then repeat the amazing outcome aloud to yourself, with conviction, at least five minutes daily. Feel it as completely true.

Set aside a special time each day to repeat your affirmations. Patterns of thought that you establish during waking hours will continue to operate on a subconscious level while you sleep. This turns out to be a significant benefit of evening sessions, though mornings, too, are good. When you awaken refreshed, your mind is more receptive to thought patterns and better able to concentrate on and receive new information.

Put yourself into the position to receive affirmations. Again, see yourself as having already obtained what you want. While holding the image, bring to mind the feelings of having fully realized your intention. Being non-critical, your subconscious will believe your visualizations as actual. The more evocative the image, the better the response. As you affirm, the subconscious will raise to your awareness images and sensations of your success.

You may want to begin each affirmation statement with words that establish the sense of something already done: *I am...*or *I am grateful that I am...*or *For the highest good of all concerned, I am....* Some more examples: *With gratitude, I am clear and courageous in all my choices. I am in perfect sync with my life-affirming expression.*

This is the process. You hold life-affirming words, thoughts, and images in your mind, and you manifest a reality that your heart desires.

Obviously, the creation and use of affirmations is a continuous process. As our intentions are realized, we affirm for the new intention. There is, however, a category of affirmations that has a specialized use. I call it a "word sanctuary."

There are several kinds of sanctuaries: an actual, physical space; an imaginary place; and a belief that serves as a refuge. They each work toward deliverance. Most of us have—or want to have—a clear sense of our "real" self. If we had to put it into words, it would be a life-affirming truth statement or prayer from deep inside. We know it and know that we know it. Like a private, peaceful place, when we go there—think it, whisper it—we have a deeper sense of peace, ease, relief, or release.

Your sanctuary is such a word or phrase—a belief you hold about yourself and your connection to all that is. It involves one of the age-old parameters through which humanity has come to find meaning. When life seems to be raging, your sanctuary assures you that peace enfolds the storm. And so you give this word or phrase or statement to yourself as your truth; let it be your daily word. When you repeat it, you are replacing anything in your mind, conscious or unconscious, that blocks this knowing. Examples: *Infinite Spirit is taking care of me,* or *May I live in peace.*

Affirmation and Sanctuary Exercises

1. If you are already in the throes of an ending, or if you are ready to let go of something in your life that has come to an end, creating a new mind-support may be your next consideration. What if whatever you need to do was already done, and done successfully? How would you feel? Consider creating an affirmation that supports you right now:

> *For the highest good of all concerned, whatever needs to be released falls away.*
>
> *In gratitude, I lovingly let go of all limitations to my highest good.*

2. If you are not aware of a belief you hold that is foundational to your sense of sanctuary, or if you want to establish another, allow one to come up, one that you want to know unequivocally. Write out your sanctuary statement, phrase, or word on a 3 x 5 card, and carry it with you to be handy whenever you need it. As you use it, you allow yourself expanded awareness of a spiritual system of which you are a part.

3. Practice letting go of things. Survey your rooms, closets, drawers, and cabinets, appraising material objects—clothing, accessories, household items, books—that you have had for some time. Be grateful for what they have brought to your life. Do you need them, treasure them? Lovingly, let go of any that no longer serve you. Notice the order and space they leave behind.

4. Create an "endings" ritual. Collect smooth stones, symbolic of completions you have experienced. You may want to inscribe them with words that capture the essence of an ending, or leave them unmarked. Use them in potted plants to support new life, or return them to the earth or to the river where they—symbolic of life's many small endings—are a part of the flow.

Truth is by nature self-evident.
—Gandhi

3

TUNING IN TO THE SACRED WITHIN

When I divorced, I had freed myself. I believed that I occupied the moral high ground: I had once been a victim, now I was a survivor. From such a vantage point, I must have seen that time as a plateau: *Now I can breathe.*

Or perhaps I saw it as a destination: *I survived. End of story.* Either way, none of us wants to risk going back to sleep. Rumi, the 13th-century poet, said it beautifully: "The breeze at dawn has secrets to tell you. / Don't go back to sleep. / You must ask for what you really want. / Don't go back to sleep." You have to keep to the idea that genuine living is what you really want.

After my transition, I expected to find a resting place, a neutral bridge marking the end of one way of life before a new way appeared on the horizon. But if living means beginning anew, how do you know when you've crossed the bridge into the new beginning? Nothing I experienced was so clear-cut.

I had three sons and a daughter. My children—ranging from the age of primary school to navigating teenage years—were bright and extraordinarily perceptive, but they were still children, trying to survive their own childhoods with hearts and minds intact. We were in this together. In them I found both inspiration and anchor. I had the single-handed responsibility of pulling this off.

Though we had a decent roof, decent food, and tolerable clothing, the supply of anything aside from that was extra, and extras were meager. A major-big-deal dog from the shelter and a gently used television one Christmas come to mind. The only thing I had resembling a time-out was my focus on keeping my head down and my nose to the grindstone. I may not have excelled in the work of a marriage, but I knew that raising children meant doing your best to see that they thrive.

My career as a medical technologist was my saving grace. By the time the drawn-out, three-year divorce was behind me, I had worked in a clinical setting for fifteen years, and I had liked the work. For most of those years, I worked in clinical hematology, where you ferret out pathologies like anemia and leukemia by studying the cellular elements of blood and bone marrow. We sorted out indicators of infectious diseases, a paramount case in point being the detection of the cells in the process that came to be known as HIV/AIDS. I considered it indispensable work that supported the diagnostic side of medicine.

If you're a conscientious worker, you're always available for overtime. You punch the time clock, collect your biweekly pay, and stretch it further than it should go. Imperceptibly, a year can stretch into four.

Like every other mother in the neighborhood, you make meals, do the laundry, clean the house, supervise homework, and enjoy a creative moment with school projects. Unlike the other mothers, you are a divorced mom scouting out the lowest echelons of discount grocery stores and combing through thrift shops. You learn how to change the tires and oil and belts of the car, prime the walls of a room before you paint it, measure and cut the right gauge for the hole in the screen door, put together a do-it-yourself shed out back, set mouse traps, freeze every dab of leftovers, and bounce checks for a few ballet lessons or football equipment fees.

Some things were solid for me—health-care benefits, for instance. Some things were not. The dryer, a window, the lawn mower, a light switch, the oven, a bicycle, the alternator, roof, fence, furnace—name it, it broke. Repairs cost money; money was short; repairs fell short. Job or no job, the old specter of poverty began to hang out in the sagging corners.

Still, I was somewhere between competent and excellent at what I did, and I moved up the ranks. A promotion to section head meant more flexibility and more money. Then, chief technologist and supervisor, the highest rungs on the short ladder to the low ceiling. Once I arrived there, the future stretched out before me in an endless string of days, distinguishable only by the occasional microscopic discovery of a rare cell or titrating the extreme level of some particular enzyme that spelled out a life sentence for some poor soul.

Bad can get worse until meaningful engagement seems doubtful in a job that is simply a paycheck. Fulfillment? Impossible. You know when some vital part of you is dying. Nothing excites you. The world is too small, and the city might as well be a maze of strip malls. You don't fit anywhere, and you don't care. Friends chatter endlessly. Eating is something to be endured. You once had a favorite song, but you don't bother with music anymore. Jokes sound stupid, people are unkind, and you don't remember your dreams, the sleeping or the waking kind. There is nothing that can stir that vital something back to life.

Though I could not see it then, there was more expression in me than could flow through my "job" channel. What I knew about the vast arena of fulfillment was limited to knitting together lofty ideas about awareness and lowly ideas about what to make for dinner. And so I did my best to figure out what was mine to do, and what was far beyond my human hands.

Aside from having more money, I found it difficult to imagine what a good life would look like. Was this what I was supposed to be doing for the rest of my life? Why was I here on earth anyway? Adrift from the old moorings, how could I resort to prayer?

In my purse I carried around a copy of a poem by James Kavanaugh, a former priest. It begins: "I have lost my easy God—the one whose name / I knew since childhood / I knew his temper, his sullen outrage / his ritual forgiveness. He was a good God—so he told me—a long-suffering and manageable one..."

My own easy God was gone. No longer could I conjure the up-there Lord I had counted on to make my life work; the one who, keeping tabs on my mistakes and good-faith offerings, would give me thumbs-up or -down on Judgment Day. Although I had forsaken those familiar interpretations, an uneasiness set off my need to come to some kind of terms with my beliefs about the sacred.

One of my sisters put me on to a book called *The Finding of the Third Eye* by Vera Alder. I had never deeply studied the mystical foundations of the religions I had subscribed to, nor had I investigated things spiritual. Limited experience, however, had led me away from any felt connection between the religious world and the world of things spiritual.

Religion had been the domain of a nebulous but supreme anthropomorphic figure, all-powerful, sometimes wrathful, in charge of my life. His rules were my religion. I had known about God, but couldn't identify anything that I would call a "God" experience. I didn't believe that I had ever experienced getting "happy" at church, nor had I ever spoken in tongues. Prayer had been the only connection I knew, and it was always me talking to Him, hoping. My obedience to His will was supposed to be my lifeline. It had been spelled out to me by an institutional church, through regular men with booming voices, big cars, and clay feet, and it was subject to their interpretation of ancient scriptures. No mysticism there.

Also I had known about his "only-begotten" son who was crucified and underwent resurrection and full-bodied ascension to a heaven beyond the sky. I had never felt in major debt for his dying, though I had given lip service to living according to His word about who was blessed in the biblical beatitudes. Before I had understood that Christ was not his last name, I had accepted the idea of Him as a personal savior in a rote, precautionary way that never touched my heart the way that, say, gospel music had touched my heart.

Whether or not Jesus's history was actual or his biography accurate, His message of love did indeed resonate with me. He was a window through which I could see something akin to the divine. Turning that into dogma, though, was another story. When I had fallen in love with the romance of ritual communion, I had understood what was being celebrated in Catholic mass, but it had all remained intellectual. On the other hand, things in the "spirit" world had had to do with a dubious realm. From childhood, I had held on to the suggestion of dark forces of the psychic or occult. When my mother had gone to Miss Porter and had certain things spelled out to her about the cause of her suffering; when, carefully, she had rolled ruined nylon stockings, or threshed hair from the hair brush, or wadded used Kotex and wrapped them in layers of newspaper, before stuffing it all into the trash drum, striking several matches to make sure that they burned to formless ashes—this was more than the simple discarding of trash; it was protection from powers in the spirit world.

Icons buried in strategic places, powders or potions sprinkled about—as I came of age none of it continued to frighten me seriously, but the root of it still related to a belief in a dark force. It was all about an energy other than divine, and unrelated to religion except in its antagonism to Christianity. The terms "psychic," "occult," and "mystical," then, seemed interchangeable. With lingering concerns about some other force having power in my life, I gave a wide berth to all things occult. They were nothing to play with.

Later, as I came into my own experiences and insights, I believed that people did actually develop faculties that defied scientific explanation. But that was a far cry from my early understanding.

And so I read this book, *The Finding of the Third Eye*, about a system of vision that went beyond the senses. After that I was propelled into an entire metaphysical genre of books, from Edgar Cayce to Paramahansa Yogananda, from the popular *Jonathan Livingston Seagull* to the underground *The Lazy Man's Guide to Enlightenment*; from *Life and Teachings of the Masters of the Far East* to a study of meditation called *The Open Way*. I inhaled them, and over time I came away with a hodgepodge meditation that—to me—was unlike the prayer I had known. It was a real silence within me.

With quiet time next to impossible in our house, my car and the bathroom became meditation spaces. I no longer considered myself religious, yet I kept to this spiritual practice religiously. There was nothing earth-shattering about it. By no means did my life seem to become easier. Still, meditation seemed to quiet some part that was always jumping up and down. If I had had the language then, I would have described the experience as one of "being more present in my life." But at the time, I probably described it as "staying with myself" as opposed to "going out of myself." I found it practical in its mystery. The urge to be consciously on a so-called path to enlightenment was overtaking the urge to continue on a so-called journey toward everlasting life. I had yet to connect the two.

I came across a broadside of "Desiderata," and taped it to my bedroom wall: "Go placidly among the noise and haste," it said, "...and remember what peace there may be in silence." And it also said, "be gentle with yourself. You are a child of the universe, no less than the trees and the stars. You have a right to be here." I seized those two passages, and especially loved the one about being a child of the universe. It transported me in memory to something strange that had occurred when I was seven or eight years old, something that I had never reconciled.

One sultry summer night when I had still been young enough not to be fazed about sleeping outside in my underpants, our mother had allowed us to drag our covers off the bed and sleep in the moist grass of our front yard. In our little corner of Wyandotte County, streetlights in designated neighborhoods were turned off at nine o'clock. When we were lucky enough to convince our mother that we would be more likely to behave ourselves in the pitch dark than in porch light, my brother, sister, and I would stay awake whispering way past nine.

I had always been fascinated by the summer night sky—
the canopy, the Big and Little Dippers, Orion. My version of
the cosmos had been as good as any other. In the dark, with
no need to fill rational gaps, I sometimes imagined the sky as
a suspension of stars in a viscous space. But this one night the
sky had been neither a finite dome nor a suspension.

I don't know how long I lay staring into the riddle of a star-
pocked sky. But suddenly I fell upwards. Without a thrust
or tug, I fell into the sky. It was as if I had blinked out of
existence. I was nowhere and everywhere. Instantaneously
the whole universe was me; I was it, everything, yet I had no
body. There was no euphoria or bliss; simply a no-thing-ness.

Though I don't remember ever talking to an adult about
my experience, I also don't remember being particularly perplexed about it. It had nothing to do with anything I understood. It was merely something strange that happened to me
when I was eight.

In later years, I spent many moments, many a night on a
stretch of earth away from city lights, staring into the magnificence of a starry sky, hoping that it might trigger that
experience. Meditation on the heavens never became my
sure-thing opening to oneness with all that is. The clarity and
primordial sense of that experience, though, never left me.

There was one particular passage in "Desiderata" that
proved to be unsettling: "Keep interested in your career, however humble; it is a real possession in the changing fortunes of
time." So I was supposed to remain interested in my career.

As a way to express my dismay at all the challenges facing
me and tease out answers, I had acquired the habit of writing
in a journal each night before bed. In my journal, I didn't
write in the stiff, scientific jargon that filled my days. I said
what I said without a thought to how I said it, and I found

myself writing in the tropes and rhythms that most naturally came to mind, the way I spoke when I wasn't trying, as if I were talking to my sister. This journal writing—where I talked to myself in my own voice about what I understood life to be—was to become a personal lifeline.

Once a dream had spoken peace to me. It had been a definite promise that I hadn't forgotten. I wanted some of that peace now; I wanted something new, something more, something better. I wanted to feel engaged in my job again, and at the same time double my paycheck. Yet even that would not be sufficient; I couldn't see how it would satisfy the thing within me that needed to stand up in the world; the part of me that needed to speak though I had nothing in particular to say, nothing to aspire to, nothing to show; the part that was always pushing to shout, *Hey, I'm here!* I felt like I was waiting for my real life. I was open to a dream, a book, a still, small voice, a grain of sand—anything that would help me to realize a way forward.

There are times when you come upon a piece of knowledge or information, and you grasp that you've uncovered a kernel of Truth. Your tiny hope of finding something to hold onto has paid off. The perception of being on a path can come from these "moments of truth" in which you're shown a way of connecting the dots that expand your idea of reality. Such moments are strung together in a rosary of grace, each gem a revelation.

For me, *The Nature of Personal Reality*, a "Seth" book by Jane Roberts, was such a moment. For one thing, Roberts uses the term "All There Is," which I took to be the consummate expression for an absolute higher energy that wasn't called "God." I did not grasp that it could mean that there is nothing else at all, ever, anywhere. I thought about it more as the mystery—a "whatever there is." And so I set aside my confusion about a limited, anthropomorphic entity, and for a time I gave the word "God" a smaller space in my vocabulary.

Roberts discussed the "present moment" as the only point of power in our lives, and insisted that true religion was incapable of repression. The chapters entreated you to say yes to life and accept your own uniqueness. Stirring stuff for me.

Most compelling—ultimately what boggled my hold on the idea of a finite reality—was her pronouncement that thought is creative. Whether or not it is what we hunger for, what we hold in mind becomes our experience. Belief is how the invisible becomes visible. Whatever we focus on grows. On some level, it made sense to me, and the mystery of *how*, and by what natural or scientific law, was not important.

As an instructive example, she takes apart the details of a burglary: a victim's house is robbed by a perpetrator. In explaining the principle involved, she points to the act itself as a merging of energy brought about by shared beliefs—those of the victim, and those of the perpetrator.

I could see that. Say the victim holds a belief about greed, or about the innate evil nature of human beings, or perhaps the victim holds a fear that no one is safe from another person's aggression. If the perpetrator then holds similar beliefs, they each will create the event—two reactions to the same set of beliefs, like attracting like. It didn't square with the scientific law about opposites attracting each other, but I got the drift of it. If I install bars on my doors and windows, I am acting on my belief not in safety, but in peril. And peril, or at least the sense of it, is what I will experience.

The nature of personal reality was that we have always created, co-created, or manifested experience, and for most of us, most of the time, we have done it unconsciously.

And so I began to contemplate in earnest the suggestion that if I was to have the life I wanted, I'd have to have positive thoughts about that life, come up with pictures of it. Thoughts gel into beliefs, and the beliefs support the desire. Theoretically at least, this was revolutionary. Belief was key. Perhaps it was my grounding in science that challenged me to test it.

All over my life, I was steeped in the sense of lack. The cause seemed clear—there were no other hands to help me, no dependable child support. Work was the way I generated income, and there simply was not enough. I was born into the struggle to overcome poverty; I took it for granted. Why else would I be working myself to a frazzle? When I thought about the details of my life, I heard "We were poor" as a line from any childhood story I ever told. Thanks to my father, manual labor alone had kept the wolves from our door and softened the perennial shame of not-having.

For as long as I could remember, I had labored relentlessly to change that. Hard work was the only way I knew, and wasn't a good job insurance against a life of doing without? Wasn't that a belief in having, and not a belief in lack?

But I could not have it both ways. Lack was what I saw. The question was whether my seeing was actually due to my internalized belief about lack. Intellectually, I understood the words, but my mind wouldn't stretch completely around the idea that I was creating what I believed and believing what I saw.

Then there was the practical application. This book suggested a simple technique for changing a belief: decide on one thing you want to work to change. Then, for five minutes each day, focus your mind entirely on the new reality—feel it, visualize it, speak it in words as if it were already true.

After five minutes, perform one physical gesture as if the new reality has already unfolded. For someone living in poverty, such a gesture might be to give away a few pennies, or pay a few cents more for the purchase of a loaf of bread than you might have been willing to pay before.

I hadn't given away any money, but I had been wrestling with this idea for months. Day in and day out, I had been confronted with the "proof" of the situation before my eyes, and could not muster the feeling of a more abundant life.

Many a night I had fallen on my bed and, for five minutes, thinking that I might as well try, I had whispered to myself, "I am wealthy." The best picture I had come up with was one of me receiving a check for a large sum of money, and sighing in relief. But of course, no suggestion of wealth had insinuated itself into my bank account.

In the throes of need one day, I was on my way to my local library with both figurative and literal gas tanks close to empty. I always went there to rent popular audios, and that day I was probably aiming for something like Al Jarreau singing "We Got By," or perhaps Roberta Flack singing "I Told Jesus [It Would Be All Right if He Changed My Name]."

Imagine sitting in your car in the parking lot of the library, a few dollars in your purse, and it's autumn. You have four children. Your gas furnace will be called into service for the chilly nights to come, and the gas in your house has been turned off for non-payment. You don't have the lump sum to cover the staggering, way-past-overdue bill and reconnection charge. You're distraught and unable to concentrate on your library mission, so you swallow the lump in your throat, forget the music, forget the library, back out of the parking lot, and take yourself home.

At home I took in the mail, deliberately ignoring the window of tinted paper that spelled out collection notices. But one thin envelope with a window stood out. It appeared to be a check. I opened it and unfolded the letter from the insurance company informing me of an error. For an extended period of time, I had been overpaying an insurance installment. Enclosed was a refund check that amounted to a few dollars more than the large balance of my gas bill.

Common knowledge has it that when flying an airplane, the pilot is never flying in a straight line at a particular altitude. Instead, continually, the pilot gets feedback from onboard instruments to inform him or her that he or she is flying "on course" or "off course." The pilot makes the necessary adjustments. As far as I was concerned, the universe had sent me an "on course" message. The message was, yes, the check in the mail had had something to do with how intensely I had held that image in my mind. I concluded that my thinking had had something to do with my life.

As the saying goes, there is nothing new under the sun, and in his wit, the writer Ambrose Bierce adds an interesting twist: "There is nothing new under the sun, but there are lots of old things we don't know." It seems every generation tinkers with the already-invented wheel. Among things not known to me then, and not known in many quarters today, are the roots of ideas that extend back through the ages.

At the time I first encountered ideas in *The Nature of Personal Reality*, I came away with only what I was capable of accepting at the time. First published in the 1970s, the book echoes principles prominent in the New Thought Movement that had flourished a hundred years earlier. In the late 1800s, a philosopher, inventor, and healer by the name of Phineas Quimby claimed that his only personal power was in understanding the error in the patient's belief and replacing it with the divine—spiritual—truth. The patient's changed mind was the cure. Quimby became the recognized "father" of the New Thought Movement. William James called it the "mind-cure" movement. It was explored and developed by prominent thinkers over time, and became a combination of philosophy, religion, and science.

Some of the most significant points were: Infinite Intelligence, or God, or whatever power by whatever name, is omnipotent, omniscient, omnipresent, and indwells each person. Spirit is the ultimate reality. Mental states are carried forward into manifestation, and become our experience. Right thinking has a healing effect.

You can find ancient roots of these ideas in the biblical "Be ye transformed by the renewal of your mind" and "Whatever you sow, that shall you also reap." From the Kabbalah, "Three are the dwellings of the sons and daughters of Man. Thought, feeling, and body. When the three become one you will say to this mountain 'move' and the mountain will move." And from the more modern Emerson—"What you are comes to you. Once you make a decision, the universe conspires to make it happen"—to the more modern Einstein: "Energy cannot be created or destroyed; it can only be changed from one form to another."

The New Thought Movement

Ultimately, New Thought emerged as general body comprising major religious denominations and spiritual groups, as well as secular organizations. Today, Unity, founded by Charles and Myrtle Fillmore; and Religious Science, founded by Ernest Holmes, are the two largest groups within the movement.

Creative thought assumes that the universe is a spiritual system: everything is part of a single unity, sprung from—and of the same nature as—its creator. It follows that everything is connected; we are a collective.

In this, you can find influences from a similar movement that flourished in 1840s New England. Central to Transcendentalism, as it was called, was the belief in a reality higher, and with greater intelligence, than human intelligence. The Transcendentalists had a core belief in the power of thought and in an ideal spiritual state that transcends the physical and empirical. Their principles were based on the dual reality, the spiritual essence of humans. The most notable Transcendentalists, Ralph Waldo Emerson and Henry David Thoreau, acknowledged indebtedness to ancient Hindu scriptures. In the ancient Upanishads from centuries before the Common Era, you can find these principles. For example, "Not that which the eye can see, but that whereby the eye can see: know that to be Brahman, the eternal, and not what people here adore. Not that which the ear can hear, but that whereby the ear can hear: know that to be Brahman, the eternal, and not what people here adore. Not that which speech can illuminate..."

The idea that there is a common denominator—a universal wisdom tradition that recurs throughout the world's religious, spiritual, and philosophical history in itself—has persisted. For centuries, deliberation and polemics have shed light on an enduring set of insights that recur over time, independent of epochs, geographies, cultures, and peoples.

The term "perennial philosophy" first appeared in writings by Agostino Steuco, a 16th-century theologian. It became established by the German philosopher Leibniz. In the contemporary era, it was popularized by Aldous Huxley in the publication of his mid-20th-century book *The Perennial Philosophy*. Depending upon interpretations of the timelessthread idea, and interpretations of Huxley's fertile writings, there are four to seven essentials of the philosophy. Whether or not they represent "Truth" to those who read them, they point to ponderings and conclusions about fundamental mysteries that have plagued and inspired humanity in every generation. In general, they explore several subjects.

- **Ultimate Reality:** This is explored as the non-physical ground of being that gives rise to the world of space and time, visible and invisible, present and transcendent. It is given many names—Life Force, Divine Spirit, Spirit, Brahman, Energy, Tao, God, the Universe, the Infinite, Divine Matrix, Nirvana, Infinite Presence, Higher Power, Source, etc. Ultimate Reality is indescribable, but has many labels— oneness, eternal, absolute, infinite intelligence, transcendent, immanent, single unity, one mind, one life, omnipotent, omniscient, omnipresent, etc.

- **Knowledge:** As human beings we have the capacity to recognize the existence of an ultimate ground of being, and also to become aware of our essence as the same nature as the Ultimate.

- **The Nature of Humans:** Life is defined as being both finite, as in the physical body, and eternal, as in pure spirit or energy. Humans have the freedom of choice to identify with either or both.

- **The Purpose of Life:** The end result of living is the uniting of our essence with the ultimate. Once we are at one with it or believe that we are, our purpose for being is served, and our life situation is new, more, better.

Over eons, mystics, scientists and philosophers have shared these insights about the nature of reality, and belief has evolved. In contemporary times, the universal, enduring set of insights increasingly resonates in mainstream thought. A ground-of-being energy that gives rise to the single unity that includes all of humanity and dwells in each individual, the power of creative thought, innate goodness—these are no longer strange ideas.

Think of evolution in its broadest sense. Developments in nature, in biology, in technology, in culture are continuously reflected upon in terms of underlying principles and possible purpose. So it is with the evolution of our perceived raison d'être. Scientists work out probabilities and possibilities, explain the laws of physics. Non-scientists observe demonstrations and rely on experience and perception. All of us are usually convinced of the veracity of natural laws such as gravity and electricity by their effects. When we can demonstrate and observe effects, we buy into the principle. So we have always possessed the capacity to realize certain things about life, whether we recognize that capacity as awakening, happenstance, revelation, or growing up. Some sense a connection between self and cosmos through study and contemplation. The infallibility of science has convinced others. For still others, it is the sudden recognition of the miraculous human body, an answered prayer, or heightened encounters with nature. Spontaneously, you can find yourself outside of time as you chop vegetables for a meal, or polish the wood-grain of a table.

Think of children. Long before they are aware of labels, they sense the essence of, say, a leaf or pebble. Things that we adults assign to the inexplicable are taken in by children as the way the world works, the way life actually is. Sometimes at the point in life when a profound question arises, the answer can lie waiting to be remembered.

And yet, can we really know the fullness of what is? Self-awareness may incline you toward awareness of a sacred self, but does it insure a fundamental shift in that direction? No one can bestow awareness on anybody else. Always, a mystery will remain. It makes sense that a creation, us, cannot encompass its creator, an ultimate. A creation is, however, an expression of its creator; it carries an essence of its maker, resembling its author in significant, albeit sometimes unrecognizable, ways.

Though the life situations with which we struggle are linked to belief, we cannot learn by rote that thought is creative. We can be open to the possibility, and consider having an experience. Whether we relegate the idea of creative thought to the realm of science, spirituality, religion, or none of the above, it is widely accepted that our perception rules our life. In large part, our minds keep us in a closed circle of seeing what we believe, and believing what we see. Much of our mental activity is generated by our drive to gather evidence to support what we believe to be true. What we create turns out to be an arc in that circle.

It is ours not to go back so sleep. It is ours to be grateful for the birthright of awareness, whether or not it seems to align with what we think we know. When a moment of truth registers, it is a moment when the world—or our version of it—shifts. In fact, as we move in what we know and understand, nothing new actually occurs. Instead, the shift is in our vision; we see differently. What changes is our awareness of what already is.

Cultivating the Practice of Meditation

Meditation is a state of being, not a state of doing anything, getting or achieving anything, or going anywhere. It is being aware—and awareness means being awake to the immediate moment, the now. In this state, you realize that you are alive: one with living, with access to all of what that means. Every now and then, spontaneously, we experience such a moment of awareness. Usually it is brief, and later—if we try to explain it—we end up using words and phrases like "peaceful," "mystical," or "peak experience." Consider a moment's experience with an awesome vista, a sunrise, a newborn child.

There are many approaches to the practice of meditation. If you have already established a deliberate meditative practice, this might be a good time to recommit to meditating daily, or being more open to the present moment.

Sampling "Now" Moments

If you are new to meditation, for now consider simply noticing "now" moments that can serve as previews to the main attraction. Rather than dwelling in yesterday or tomorrow, in any moment, you can be aware of the present—the only moment that you are actually in—by realizing where you are and what you are doing, and, eventually, what you are thinking. Loading the dishwasher, examining a melon at the market, brushing your teeth, stepping off a curb—just say to yourself, *Now I am squeezing the cantaloupe,* and so forth. Instantaneously, for a fleeting microsecond, you come into awareness of the moment you're in. *Now I am stepping onto the escalator. Now I am turning the steering wheel. Now I am breathing in.* After some practice, you will find that you need not finish the sentence in order to experience a little shift. Saying the word "now" will do.

When you are with others, try "coming present" by saying, *This moment is for me.* After more practice, no words will be necessary. Having the intention to be present will introduce you to living more in the "now" moment.

Consider a few more simple coming-present moments:

- Walk down the street and feel the breeze across your cheek.
- Listen to the white noise of an automatic heating or cooling unit, and notice your awareness when it clicks off.

    ☛ Catch the moment of sunrise or moonrise at any horizon and allow whatever comes.

    ☛ Gently touch a new leaf on a tree.

The Main Attraction

By definition, meditation is a devotional exercise or mind-body practice that trains the mind and brings calm, clarity, and a peaceful state. This process of alert awareness allows the practitioner to be present rather than being lost in thought about the past or the future. You can go beyond the mind's limitations and become still enough to experience Stillness, silent enough to experience Silence, available to experience a heightened awareness of your own spiritual dimension, your oneness with all that is.

Devotion can bestow mind-body gifts. In their book, *Buddha's Brain: The Practical Neuroscience of Happiness, Love, and Wisdom,* neuropsychologist Rick Hanson and neurologist Richard Mendius explain the science behind many mind-body benefits of a regular practice of meditation, which include greater levels of relaxation and body awareness, improved attention, and improved compassion and empathy. Hanson and Mendius explain how meditation acts on the brain to lift mood, decrease stress-related hormones, strengthen the immune system, and improve a variety of health-related conditions, including heart disease, diabetes, and chronic pain. Given these positive effects, meditation is a popular prescription with health-care professionals.

As a process to promote spiritual growth, meditation has been practiced all over the world. Tribal shamans of indigenous cultures have used it for centuries. Actual beginnings are lost in antiquity, but it is usually agreed that earliest forms came from Hindu traditions in ancient India.

Other forms developed among the Chinese, the ancient Israelites, the Byzantines, the Islamic Sufis, and the Christian saints. In more modern times, the meditation aspects of Buddhism and Hinduism, along with various forms of yoga, were introduced in the West.

Most religions have meditative practices; Buddhist Mindfulness meditation, Zen meditation, and Transcendental meditation come to mind, as do yoga, qigong, and tai chi. As a tool for turning attention from the outer and focusing on the inner, most forms share a common outcome—the experience of a relaxed, alert, heightened state of awareness, the stillness that underlies all.

Most techniques emphasize the noticing of, and non-attachment to, whatever arises, and use a centering process that enhances the tendency to allow while minimizing the tendency to try. Breath, mantras, objects, movements, thoughts that arise—all become the thing that holds attention. Paying attention to the base thought, sound, movement, or object, however, is not the goal of meditation. Rather, as you center down, you allow transcendence of the mind and attainment of expanded awareness.

Depending on the practice you choose, you carry out simple or complex steps daily. You'll find countless books, classes, and various other scholarly and spiritual sources that stress a few general requirements: a physical and mental space free of distractions; an alert, comfortable body posture; a focused mind; an effortless, non-judgmental approach; a surrender to awareness.

When choosing a practice, you'll want simplicity, ease, and what feels most natural. In order to find a good fit if you're new to meditation, you may want to try one technique for a period of time, then another. Find a simple reference text that offers useful modes and techniques, such as Roy Eugene Davis's *An Easy Guide to Meditation*, Ram Dass's *Journey of Awakening: A Meditator's Guidebook*, Thich Nhat Han's *Peace Is Every Step: the Path of Mindfulness in Everyday Life*, or Sharon Salzberg's *Real Happiness: The Power of Meditation*.

Joy, bliss, peace—whatever label you wish to apply to coming into stillness is a result of being beyond the mind's busy machinations. As we come to know that another state is always available, we bring this to our daily lives, enabling more clarity, more calm, stronger focus, and less stress. We begin to see the sacred in everything and everyone.

Meditation Modes

Initially, my biggest challenge with mediation was relaxing enough to let my body breathe without controlling my breath. For a very long time, that didn't work for me. I didn't seem to be able to breathe without taking over control of my breathing. I ended up with a self-made mantra. The takeaway from that trial time was that techniques are subjective; you do what works for you. At one time, a mantra was what worked for me.

We say that meditation is an opportunity to let go of problems, memories, and imaginings for a period, and turn inward. You remain alert and attentive, yet without striving to achieve or acquire anything, or trying to go anywhere. We say, just allow the stillness or being-ness that is beyond the limits of your mind.

Now, for a moment, let go of all that. Forget that you intend to meditate. Instead, let your intention be to let your body breathe itself. Let whatever it is that keeps your breathing going automatically breathe while you watch. Learning to observe your breath without controlling it is good practice for learning to observe your mind without controlling it. And learning to observe your mind without controlling it is great practice for being in the present moment, letting go of your "story," letting everything be as it is, and letting everyone be as they are.

Meditation Exercises

1. The following basic steps can guide you into becoming the observer.

- Set aside time for observing your breath. Twenty minutes is a good period.
- Diminish sensory distractions as much as possible. Dim any bright lights, turn off any loud sounds, make still any activity.
- Sit upright in a comfortable posture, with comfortable support for your body. A chair, sofa, or pillow on the floor will do. Being alert is a part of focusing; it is not recommended that you lie down. Close or lower your eyes.
- Take a deep breath, relax, and take three or four more deep breaths, filling your lungs all the way up from bottom to top, belly to chest. As you exhale, let go of any sensory distractions, any distress or concern. Drop your shoulders. Allow the chair to support the weight of your body.
- Now allow your breath to return to its normal rhythm.
- Now slowly scan each part of your body and release any tension you find there: from toes to ankles, to calves, to knees, to thighs, to genitals and buttocks, to belly, to chest, to arms and hands, to shoulders, to neck, to chin and cheeks, to mouth to ears, to forehead and top of the head.
- Notice your breathing. Think of your breath as originating low in your abdomen. Observe and focus on the automatic rise and fall of your belly. If it is beneficial to you, focus on feeling your breath pass into your nostrils as you inhale. Feel it pass out of your nostrils as you exhale. Let it do what it does on its own. Or, if it is beneficial, count your breaths on

the exhale with a long *onnnnne, twoooooo*, and so forth, up to ten. Then begin again with one.

~ If awareness comes, let it be; surrender to it. When your awareness strays, no need to judge, just return it to the focal point of your breath. Relax and allow

~ When the time comes to an end, sit for a few moments re-orienting yourself to your physical environment.

2. The following, a simple meditative practice of being with what is, may demonstrate the challenge of simply allowing yourself to be as you are in any moment.

~ Set aside a time and quiet place for a 20-minute period.

~ Situate your body upright in a comfortable position, with a comfortable support—a chair or a pillow on the floor.

~ Close or lower your eyes.

~ Take a deep breath: inhale, filling your lungs from the bottom to the top, inflating belly to chest. At the top of the inhalation, hold your breath for a few seconds, then exhale slowly from top to bottom, and, as you exhale, drop your shoulders and allow the chair to support your body. Repeat this three more times.

~ Breathe normally.

~ Scan your body and release any tension you find in any part.

~ Now relax. Don't be concerned about focus. Give yourself permission just to *be*. Allow your mind to do whatever it does without judging it. Busy monkey dashing from thing to thing, still water, memory, fantasy, imagination—everything is allowed. If awareness happens, so be it, and if not, so be it.

~ After 20 minutes, gently stop letting yourself be. Notice if there is a lingering sense of freedom. Then go on with living as best you can. Growth and expansion are a part of your natural state. Let fear be fear, peace be peace.

3. Consider the use of a mantra as a centering choice that allows awareness beyond the busyness of your mind. A mantra is a specific syllable, word, sound, or phrase used in meditation. Certain words qualify as mantras because they are believed to have a certain frequency vibration. Very often, a name for God suffices. Mantras can be silent or audibly chanted. Silent or aloud, they are always a monotone—no more than one or two notes—and always repetitive. When used silently, the manta becomes as an ongoing hum that maintains itself deeply within you. With time, it may no longer seem to have a beginning or end.

The root sound om, pronounced "aum" ("ahhoouumm"), in the Hindu religion signifies the oneness of all creation, the sound that created the world. The syllable hu, pronounced "huuuuu," from the Sufi belief system, holds the sound of divinity, and is considered the sound of all sounds. The word "peace" is also a common divine syllable.

For meditating with the use of a silent mantra, try the following.

- Set aside time for your meditation.
- Sit upright in a comfortable position, with comfortable support—a chair or a pillow on the floor—for your body in a quiet place.
- Scan your body, and release any tension that you notice.
- Close or lower your eyes to limit sensory distraction.
- Take a deep breath, filling your lungs all the way up from bottom to top, belly to chest. As you exhale, drop your shoulders and let go of any sensory distractions, any distress or concern, for now.
- Allow the chair to support the weight of your body. Take three or four more deep breaths, and allow your breath to come back to its normal rhythm.

- Allow the mantra to come as a syllable, or as a visual. Hear it silently.
- Allow the syllable to find and maintain its own rhythm.
- When your awareness strays, bring it back to your mantra, which is ongoing, sustaining itself without end.
- Over time, the mantra goes on deeply within you as the context of all awareness.
- When your meditation comes to an end, sit for a few moments and reorient yourself to your physical environment.

The heart sees better than the eye.
—Hebrew Proverb

4

FINDING WHAT IS SEEKING YOU

Wanting to speak, needing to open to whatever wants to come, waiting to make an original mark, longing to somehow claim a place in the world—these are clues that the need for fuller self-expression is upon you, and you are becoming conscious of it. That Infinite Something is seeking expansion in you. You are seeking to become a unique channel through which Infinite Life flows into this realm.

Sometimes it comes as a need to add something to yourself in order to have value. Perhaps you're telling yourself that if you could just be more or have more, your life would work. That becomes an incentive that can take you deeper.

Another kind of incentive comes from love—what you would love to do no matter what. For example, Come hell or high water, perhaps you would love to open the perfect childcare center. I believe that I had some of both types of incentive, but one thing I know is that this most compelling urge can hold the undeniable energy of a calling; it's your heart's desire.

I like to think that I revisited the fact of my one-time desire to be free, and despite everything, I had envisioned myself as free. Because I had held to my resolve, everything I had needed to finalize a divorce had appeared. My life was proof that with my belief, I had once created at least the possibility of a life I truly wanted. But the circle is always incomplete, and the spiral is ever twirling. Just when you begin to doubt the advantages of being wherever you are, the next curve appears, and you're off into another turn.

I no longer wanted to be on a couples' journey. I no longer wanted to be unaware of dropping bombs on my own life. I no longer wanted to struggle, plod, or settle, and I no longer wanted to be without enough money. I wanted peace and ease. I wanted substance. And while I was at it, I wanted to achieve something that added beauty to my life, something that had meaning in the doing of it.

The Latin origin of the word "desire" is "from the stars." It suggests "from the Father." That channel through which we would love to bring the Infinite into this realm already exists as potential within everyone. The hunger to form what is ours from the absolute giving-ness is a call to be open to express Life.

In fact, everything expresses. To express is to be alive. Everything in space and time is giving form to the infinite current that runs through and animates all creation. Each of us has a portal within that allows that current to be out-pictured as expression. A lowly dandelion's vivid blooms and the delicate, silver tufts that follow are a way of expressing. Life expresses as wind, scattering silver parachutes of seeds right off the stem and onto the fertile ground. Every mountain and tree, every animal and insect, every human expresses Life by its own name in a way that is unique.

To express is to realize your own aliveness, and the activity of it can stir body and mind. Self-expression out-pictures your individuality, and when you embark on it, you are saying "yes" to life.

I sensed an inner portal, but I didn't have a clue about what that outlet might look like for me. I needed an answer to the question of *What?* I like to think that in the back of my mind was the rhetorical question *Why am I here?* I'm sure that I went through the morally-correct questioning of *What is mine to do?*, which would have ignored my heart altogether. *What can I do?* was as good a place to start as any. Relying on calculated aptitude, I took the Graduate Record Exam, thinking maybe I could try for a master's degree in some area of hospital administration.

As I grew up, I had not been aware of a significant talent that I could claim. Until I was much older, I had thought of creative expression as what we had done at school every Friday with watercolors while a scratchy concerto of "real" music played on the teacher's record player. Or it was what they did in junior-high art class. I always bought into the more sophisticated connotations of being "creative," associating them with being "cultured", a concept related to a certain social status. It was not lost on me that the "cultured" were always people of means. That wouldn't be me.

Throughout high school, I had sung with choruses and church choirs, and for a short time in college I had been a vocalist with a jazz combo. My excursions into the realm of music were simply incidental to me. I never pursued art in a disciplined way; therefore, I probably reasoned, my little attempts at it were not legitimate.

Legitimacy aside, any life-affirming desire to express is a portal for creativity. Everyone is creative. And so, to consciously express is to set an intention to be the director of your own creative impulse.

It is true that for a very long time "artistic" creativity was the actual subject in any conversation about the definition of the word "creativity," and in any discussion of where creativity comes from, and who the "creatives" are. The terms "creative" and "artistic", however, are not necessarily synonymous.

Think about the fundamental truth of what it means to manifest a creation. We didn't create ourselves. We are made manifest in the nature of Infinite Life. By whatever name or concept, we are Its expression. Therefore, we cannot *not* be creative. In plain and grand ways, by conscious design or blind stumbling, we are all using whatever the process is that allows an invisible no-thing to become a visible something. We feel the hunger. Disquiet will not be stilled. Deliberately, we begin the search for relief or satisfaction. We imitate the process by which we ourselves were made manifest.

We each have one or more burning interests, talents, or particular activities we can do, or a special way of doing them that is truly original. We yearn to bring into existence something that we name "work" or "invention," making known what was an unknown. Shaping something out of our own values, sensibilities, and consciousness is a way of claiming that we have just as much right to be here as the trees and the stars. Asserting our individual way of expressing Life is a way of saying "I am." And that can be in art, business, human thought, science, and an infinite number of other domains.

Without blinking, we can have moments of genius when we think or act out pure brilliance beyond anybody's rational dictates. That impulse to set forth or press out something that is inner—that is the call within us of life to life. So any life-affirming heart's desire to do this cannot be denied. Motivated by the possibility of fulfillment, and as a catalyst for it all, we get in touch with what we really want to do, be, or have.

I liked playing the guitar and had composed a few sad songs. I had tried the then-popular, airbrushed acrylic paintings on black velvet. Hobbies, I called them, and none took root. I had always had a certain intellectual regard for art and literature, but poetry remained in the realm of the esoteric, for only the select few who could master iambic pentameter and free verse at the same time. What I knew of literature as a whole was whatever I had been exposed to in high school and college as requisites for a science degree. Universal themes in the voices of people who were long dead dominated the literature I knew, and left gaping holes in my knowledge of the sacred canon of literary excellence. I was unaware that the canon was quickly changing.

Yes, there was Gwendolyn Brooks. And there was Nikki Giovanni and her contemporaries. But they were another story altogether. I obsessed over the recording of Nikki reading her poetic tribute to Aretha with a gospel choir as backup. I could mime all of Gil Scott-Heron's intonations. But Maya Angelou's *I Know Why the Caged Bird Sings*, and Ntozake Shange's *For Colored Girls*—names and titles that had come out of the Black Arts Movement while I was busy making a family—well, these were things I had never categorized.

Their work was immediate, like cell memory to me. Yet I related to them as I related to celebrities who were way out of my league. I was not the gifted activist that I saw in them. I was not a writer. I was pushing 40, too old to consider being a part of this new means of expression. I was a scientist, too set in my ways to begin again at square one.

The voice of resistance was strong, and in my quiet time I struggled to hear my heart's desire. If, out of an infinite number of potential lives, I could choose the one I wanted, what would I choose? My version of a perfect life had plenty of money at the core. Somehow I must have been blocked because this question—never mind the answer—eluded me. And so I created an affirmation. It went something like, *For the highest good of all concerned, I have perfect clarity about how to spend my time and energy in a way that brings me prosperity and fulfillment.* I ran that affirmation five minutes a day for months.

Eventually I got a clue about the thinking that had muddied the waters. I needed to move money off the table altogether. It seemed to be a separate issue. The right question emerged then, something like, *If I had more money than me and my family could ever spend, what would I do with my time and energy?* And of course the question led me to modify the picture I wanted to impress upon the universe: *For the highest good of all concerned, I have perfect clarity about how to spend my time and energy in a way that engages and fulfills me.*

Infinite potential means that your creative "thing" is already a given, and so another question might be, *How is it that we humans come to accept our creative expression?* Finding the channel is first. To ensure our receptivity, the consciousness portal within calls on faculties that come with this life. Ours is just to say yes when the thing arrives and those faculties—intuition, imagination, passion—come into play.

One Saturday night, a friend who was into the local poetry scene invited me to an open reading. Poetry readings were ubiquitous; all the Sunday papers published calendars with venues. I liked poetry well enough, and I had yet to experience a reading.

As we entered the rear of the tiny club downtown, I suppose I imagined it would be like open mic in any other club—packed with obvious amateurs out to have a good time. It was crowded; a combo played progressive jazz while folks milled around, visiting and sipping drinks. Up front, people clumped around a few tiny tables, and farther back, almost all the folding chairs in haphazard rows were taken. We found two empty seats.

My friend made her way up front to a boyish man in a black tee flaunting a clipboard, and signed up before all of the five-minute-maximum spots were gone. A sense of expectancy saturated the place.

When the man in black took over the microphone, the audience went quiet. He welcomed everyone and went through a string of coming events before he got down to announcing the night's poets. After applause and shout-outs, the first poet took his sheaf of papers to the microphone. He was followed by what seemed to be scores of women and men merging in an unforgettable experience.

Once they began I was awestruck. Surely these people were not mere amateurs. They said and did what I had not fathomed you could say and do with poems. There was love going up in smoke, injustices unaddressed, lost footing, newfound hope—all unfettered by rules. They chanted in metaphors lifted from the ordinary things I encountered every day. The pieces were too much like real life to be shoved into the stale, off-the-point category that I knew poetry to be. Each piece was more a performance than a mere reading.

I wanted to do what they were doing. The way they played with rhythm and rhyme—raw, gentle, sharp, blunt—created a tour de force of language that stood my arm hair on end. Envy, too, surged. Here I was, waking up, wanting to speak, not knowing how to do it, and here were these ordinary people shouting to their heart's content. Plain and simple, I loved the ideas, I loved the language, I loved the music, and the combination set me on fire. The fact that I was constructing my own definition of poetry was not yet conscious; I only had the feeling that *this is it!*

Will you know it when you see it? An element of home resonates when you identify your thing; a sense of "this is what I'm meant to do, what I was born to do." The authenticity of it resonates mentally, physically, and emotionally as well. You may have taken it for granted for all your life, dismissing it with "anyone can do this." You may have had it educated out of you, or the disapproval of others may have shamed it quiet.

When you're awestruck, the "practical" harness just doesn't fit, and, try as I might that night in that place, I could not dismiss the possibility of a sea change in my life.

Because creativity is always seeking a form, the promise of fulfillment is inherent in the sense of longing. You yearn to do something. An impulse turns you in an untried direction. Discovered or revealed, it becomes a heart's desire. A new idea, a clarification, or an answer to an unasked question insinuates itself into your consciousness. With an unexpected surge of wisdom, you are suspended in an elevated state, astonished to have received something out of the blue.

In the days and weeks that followed the poetry reading, even swamped with work at the hospital, when I asked myself the question about what I intended to do, the answer was a no-brainer. My answer had not come as a mere intuition or subtle revelation. Rather, it had shook me in a physical and emotional quake. If I could in any possible way, I would write poems about my own view of how it all goes on, speak my own word into the world. I would figure out how to put it all down in a form that sang itself off the page. I had only sat in on one live poetry reading and heard recordings of two poets. But any way I sliced it, I wanted to be a writer.

I didn't know how to begin, but starting with that night, I understood the term "aesthetics." It had come into view from a world parallel to mine. Soon I walked to the beat of syllables I heard in my head. I continued to journal, and gradually I discovered that, although it had been my way of figuring out where I had been and where I wanted to go, I began paying closer attention to my language. Beneath emotions spilled there, I glimpsed something not obvious to me before: certain word choices; certain rhythmic syllables.

For weeks this scattering of expression absorbed me and I pored over pages of my journals looking for sparks. Daily, sometimes even as I came awake, the self-talk would start, but the focus had shifted from complaint to sorting out ideas and playing around with language.

Among the entries, one passage stood out as a memory fraught with meaning: "There were times Mom would play the piano and sing, *Lord Jesus, can I have a talk with you?* She would always cry as if God could never answer such a need." I lifted the passage from my journal and worked for days to shape it into something I dared call a poem.

Experiences can be woven into the fabric of childhood and remain out of reach for years, until they spring up with new force, like new ideas, exploding the either-or question of nature versus nurture. One of those hundreds of Sunday mornings when our house had been alive with preparations for church, and all of us had chimed in on "The Lord Is My Shepherd," I had had a recognition of my mother's art. My stillness in the cool tub of water had been my meditation on it.

Her style had always been unique. She had always modeled it as a matter of course. Circumstances, emotions—those were raw materials. Nothing had ever been lacking. At a time when I as desperate for expression, the entirety of an impressionable childhood was available to me. I had drunk in jazz and gospel like water, and now their rhythms reverberated as my own voice.

And so, like an ancient reader poring over parchment, I mined my journals for anything that might be useful. By virtue of being a child of the universe and being my mother's daughter, I was inevitably drawn to my own creative expression. Tacked to my bulletin board was an old program from the Unitarian Church that included a quote from Goethe: "Concerning all acts of creation, there is one elementary truth...that the moment one definitely commits oneself, then Providence moves too. All sorts of things occur that would otherwise never have occurred.... Whatever you can do, or dream you can, begin it."

Quietly, I began to write poems.

There is no veil between you and the Infinite. According to an old European proverb, "God comes to see us without bell." Intuition is that faculty by which you receive ideas "out of the blue."

If, in your imagination, you allow that everything is possible, your imagination will take you where logic and reason cannot go. Those places are real, though they may not yet exist.

Passion will both get you there and sustain you. The powerful emotion, the ardent love, the enthusiasm, the object of that enthusiasm—in conscious creative expression, passion shows itself in all these ways.

When you find yourself gravitating toward what seems to come naturally to you, you automatically attract experiences that dramatize it for you. The person on stage playing the violin may be a mirror to the person who has always been fascinated by the sounds coming out of that instrument. The television announcer reflects the desire of somebody's heart. The tinkerer will dwell on the magazine image of an inventor wearing the look of complete absorption. Or a sensual memory will be the wakeup call: the exquisite texture of a grandmother's hand-woven shawl; the aroma of nutmeg and coriander.

In other words, already you occasionally vibrate at the frequency of the thing you want to do, so that you feel it humming. The quickening you feel is a response to what you already know and recognize as a part of yourself. It is like a homing device within, answering what is calling to you.

We are always moving along the spiral of possibility. When we consciously begin channeling creativity in these terms, we see shifts in awareness that point us in life-affirming directions and demonstrate our connection to all.

Beware of sabotaging yourself. Repression has consequences. The desire to express is to be ignored only at the cost of heeding what it means to be truly alive. Separating yourself from your passion is to separate yourself from all associations with it. You may experience the apparent disconnect as feeling loneliness, less than capable, like you don't fit in, or like you aren't worthy of notice. You may go down the slope into the less-than-worthwhile category that leads to a lack of well-being.

The old stories you created that framed your sense of what you can and cannot do can go on determining the rules by which you find your way through life. Or not. Those internal censors filter out guidance and support, and mistake serendipity for luck. But creative expression in itself demonstrates prosperity. Financial wealth is always a possibility, but the principles that allow you to manifest your channel of expression are the same principles that allow you to manifest every kind of wealth.

If, because you're caught up in assumptions about age, you think that the train has already left the station, know that another train will arrive. Time spent living life is gold. Nothing is ever lost.

Nobel laureate Toni Morrison was 39 when she published *The Bluest Eye*, her first novel. Singer-songwriter Andrea Bocelli, who twice won the World Music Award for Best-Selling Classical Artist and in 2010 won World's Best Classical Artist—was once a lawyer. Blind from the age of 12, he started singing seriously at age 34. Laura Ingalls Wilder was in her sixties when she published *Little House on the Prairie*. Julia Child published her first cookbook at age 49. Morgan Freeman first appeared in a feature film in his mid-forties. Imagine Charles Darwin putting together the groundbreaking *On the Origin of Species* when he was 50, and Colonel Sanders franchising Kentucky Fried Chicken at 65. Perceptions about who should be doing what at what age are unproductive. It is never the wrong time to express yourself.

Simply being dutiful—asking from the intellect *What is mine to do?*—squeezes possibilities into a narrow line. A related pitfall is limiting the choice to what you "should," "must," or "ought to" do. A more productive approach is simply to go with what you prefer. "Should," "must", and "ought to" will not motivate you to go the last mile or shift you to the mindset you want to experience. "Should" controls expression from the small, limited self, and blocks the flow that rises to the level of brilliance. Howard Thurman, the philosopher, theologian, and civil rights leader, left us this advice: "Don't ask yourself what the world needs. Ask yourself what makes you come alive, and then go and do that, because what the world needs are people who have come alive."

Preference is immune to self-judgment and the judgment of others. You can get in touch with it as long as what you want is not obscured by seeking approval or courting permission. After all, you are simply acknowledging a preference, and you are not committed to acting in one way or another, just allowing that bit of honesty with yourself. Clarity about preference brings the opportunity to actually choose. Choice is always yours, and without choice there is no real freedom. And so, in conscious creative expression, identifying and choosing the seed of the thing you want to harvest is a crucial step.

Fertile Questions

The question *What do I wish I had the courage or time to do?* can uncover all manner of filters you've been living with that don't serve you. *What would I do if I knew I could not fail?* has such resonance because it sheds light on the fear of failure and fear of success as well, either of which can change your life situation in unpredictable ways.

When you look among the things in your life that you are presently aware of, you can explore the avenues that bring contentment. And so the question is about the experience you are looking for. Is it fulfillment, joy, peace? From one perspective, it does not matter which "thing" you choose. Whether you become a videographer or an entrepreneur, that thing is a tap on the shoulder that points you in the direction that serves your ultimate purpose.

When he was three years old, Louis Braille accidentally injured his eye in his father's workshop. The injury became infectious, blinding both eyes. At a school for the blind, Braille learned to read, but he wanted the impossible. He wanted to write. His desire led him to use the same tool that had blinded him in order to devise a system of strategically placed dots that corresponded to letters of the alphabet: the Braille alphabet. He—and millions of others—could now read and write.

Annie Leibovitz was a college student studying painting at an army base in Japan. Between her first and second years of college, she began taking pictures. "For lack of anything to do," she says, "I was using the base's hobby shop, the darkroom, and starting to take pictures. I felt filled up right away."

Find what turns you on, gives you a sense of awe, and puts you in touch with your inner self. Allow what stirs an unaccustomed part of you to continue, keeping you awake at night in enthusiasm. What is it that gushes forth in ideas and strikes unforgettable images where there were none, with the inexplicable appearing everywhere? Your individual way of allowing that thing is more unique than a fingerprint. Answering some of the obvious questions I have outlined provides a way to stay open, to say to the universe, "show me." As you bring your musings to the conscious level, you ready yourself for action.

Cultivating Receptivity

If you have never known what it is to have a creative expression that touches your heart, consider identifying one now. Your thoughts, beliefs, words, actions, and attitudes—all of what you control—contribute to your receptivity to the guidance you need in order to make that choice. Nothing is ever withheld.

A useful quotation, often attributed to Albert Einstein, tells us that "the intuitive mind is a sacred gift, and the rational mind is a faithful servant. We have created a society that honors the servant and has forgotten the gift." If you make a pros and cons list when beginning a new pursuit, you may end up honoring the servant, the rational mind. You'll choose what you consider to be your excellence, or what others expect of you. If, on the other hand, you go with what you sense as your passion, you honor the sacred gift, your intuition.

Cultivating intuition is where you can demonstrate for yourself the practicality of spiritual practices. Meditation is a path that supports your openness to intuitive guidance. Journaling is vital to bringing conscious attention to intuition. Then, by acting on those impulses, you grow trust and expand the avenue for receiving answers. You can use somewhat less significant incidents and "coincidences" as baby steps. Say you're driving home on your usual route and intuition tells you to turn onto a new street altogether. Rather than overruling it with *Yes, but* or *What if?*, go with the impulse. You may discover the wisdom of the detour immediately or never, but you will be exercising the intuition muscle.

Another fertile process to help you rely on intuition is simply to pose any important questions to which you want answers. If you're in the middle of making a decision, get quiet and use your sanctuary statement to center yourself. Silently, aloud, or in your journal, ask, for example, *What will serve the greatest good here?* Then let go of your own attempts to figure it out. Expect the answer to come and be open to all avenues by which it may arrive. In your journal, record all "intuitive hits" that involve any aspect of your life.

So it is with something as significant as the question of the creative expression you yearn for. The intuitive guidance may not show up in the way you expect, so be open to seeing, sensing, feeling, and the outright smack of direct recognition. Be open, too, to the larger context that is being served— your highest good. Amazing configurations of transformative events often appear. Mind-clearing episodes, releases of blocks that you didn't know were there—all can coalesce to realign you with your intention.

Love is always the answer, and the form of it can be specific to your sensibilities and life situation. As your own discernment kicks in, the answers confirm that the act of asking is, in itself, a willingness to receive. Like a bubble of warm air, valuable information bursts into your consciousness from directions that may have once seemed foreign.

If you are simply cold or blank about what you want, a fertile resource is one originated by Dr. Michael Beckwith. He has developed a comprehensive process of revelation and set it out in an audio learning course called *Life Visioning*. He describes it as "transformational inner technology for uniquely expressing the love, wisdom, and beauty that we are." In the audio course, he says that Visioning "allows you to intuit God's idea of Itself as your life."

Janet Bray Attwood and Chris Attwood's Passion Test may be another place to begin the process of daring to dream big, going deep into your heart, and forming a genuine intention to express yourself. In the introduction their book *The Passion Test*, the authors ask what it means to live a passionate life. They answer with the superlative experiences we all seek: "fulfilling, thrilling, on fire, turned on, motivated, easy, fun, unstoppable. A life aligned with destiny." Whether or not predestined life is a part of your belief system, their book outlines a simple and productive method that can help to identify what you want for your overall living.

Receptivity Exercises

Meanwhile, remember that your conscious mind wants something to do. You can fortify that chamber so that it is preoccupied with relevant ideas that activate all your faculties. Consider any or all of the following exercises.

1. Contemplate a few rational questions and journal the insights that come:

- What do you hope you live long enough to do, or to see done?
- What are you doing when you feel most alive?
- Have you ever used materials at hand in an original way to solve a problem?
- What do you do for fun?
- How do you tinker?
- What life-affirming activity do you choose once you have done your chores, or fulfilled your obligations?
- What have you always done as a pastime? How does that fit as a lifestyle?
- Who are the people you feel drawn to? What are they doing?
- What is your idea of a great week off from work (when all your obligations are handled)?

2. Prime the pump of memory, where forgotten dreams may resurface. With journal and pen handy, consider these questions:

- As a child, what was your favorite way to play?
- What were you really good at, what did you wish you were good at, and what did people always tell you that you were good at?
- Before you were 10 years old, what—more than anything—did you want to be?
- Who was the most talented person you knew?
- What made/makes you laugh?
- What was/is one of your best habits?
- What good thing/idea/activity/moment escaped you?
- What did you let go of for some (good) reason?

- What was taken away?
- What were you always convinced was not yours to do or to pursue?
- What is the most surprising thing you have ever done?
- What would constitute your shining hour?
- Remember a very good day in your life before you were 10. Create the scene.
- Fill in the blanks: I could do what I wanted if only I had the _____ (skill, courage, ability, talent, energy, money, time, support, strength, focus, resolve) to do it.

3. Make a nametag—preferably the pendant style—that would be revealing in a future encounter with someone. Write your name, then add a title, label, or some instantly recognizable commentary that comes closest to describing your true creative expression. (Example: "Larry Cooper, Owner, Kites in the Wind.") Carry it on your person out of sight until you are ready to go public with your new intention. Here are a few suggested tags: singer, activist, negotiator, doctor, artist, musician, comedian, designer, healer, lawyer, cartoonist, caterer, plumber, journalist, clown, therapist, mechanic, entrepreneur, carpenter, performer, decorator, mathematician, counselor, stylist, painter, facilitator, governor, director, homemaker, nurse, chef, educator.

4. Create an affirmation relevant to where you are in the process of discovery. Affirm your general, conscious intention to do, to be, or to have. For example:

For the highest good, I am clear and courageous in all my choices.

I am grateful that I choose wisely and follow my intuition.

I acknowledge unlimited possibilities of expression within me.

I am grateful that everything I need to know is revealed to me.

5. Take a walk through a natural setting or cityscape, and notice that creative expression is everything, everywhere. Pay special attention to the innumerable ways in which nature expresses. Also notice human-built objects, organized institutions and programs, artistic pursuits, and scientific and technological developments.

6. On a similar walk, collect any four objects—natural or manufactured—that capture your attention. Bring them back with you, and by combining them in any way you like, create something beautiful and/or functional. This is an expression of your own sensibilities. Keep it as a symbol of your claim to being creative.

An ounce of performance is worth pounds of promises.
—Mae West

5

MAKING THE COMMITMENT

How many times has an idea invaded your imagination so fully that you ran right out and bought books, supplies, and equipment; cleared a space in the basement; made a schedule for yourself; and, self-satisfied, got right to it, telling your closest friends about your new venture? Have many times have you, months later, found yourself wondering where to store the equipment and supplies until you could get back to what it took to focus on the idea that had once so captured your imagination?

It can be tempting to linger in maybe-land, savoring the satisfaction of having made a choice, but shying away from commitment. The business of consciously committing your mind, body, and spirit to a new creative expression requires stepping up your energy over time to both develop and sustain new habits. You have to overcome the inertia of falling backwards into old patterns. You may hold an "arrival" image daily, where you reign supreme, but unless you are continuously alive with the felt experience of being there, you won't wear the crown. It must be true in you before it can be true in the world.

To feel that you are that thing involves your heart; your mind-muscle isn't strong enough to go it alone. Opening to each part of the process of becoming builds the "feeling-ness" quotient. The small ups and downs—the ends-of-this, beginnings-of-that—turn out to be the pistons in the engine of creativity.

To commit is to keep the spiritual channel open. Once you open it a little, the flow of giving-ness widens. The more you are willing to accept, the more will come your way. Your constancy in saying yes is the expansion the channel seeks.

Though Thomas Edison did not invent the first crude flash of electric light, he performed innumerable experiments with thousands of materials before he came up with a filament that would last 40 hours and give the world the first practical electric bulb. You have to keep going. In the experience of a driver traveling by car from California to New York at night, the road ahead is illuminated only a few yards at a time. Anticipating your next step is what keeps your dream new. Each time you come to a halt, the next step appears.

I knew I had come to a halt. It was ironic that Food for Thought was the name of the vegetarian restaurant where I sometimes got cheap, nutritious take-out. The shoddy, cavernous space boasted a decent menu, wooden tables, a tin ceiling, a tip jar, and community bulletin board covered with flyers that were fringed in tear-off phone numbers. As I was leaving one day, I noticed an emerald-green flyer that said something odd in bold print: "Community Poetry Workshop." I had never heard of a course that was exclusively for writing and critiquing poetry. The details on the flyer were all about encouraging and developing writers who "showed promise." Every semester, George Washington University held a free community poetry workshop led by an established writer. Eligibility for admission included non-student status and five "good poems." Since there were only ten slots open each session, this was a competition.

For more than a year, I had been scribbling in my bedroom. In my half-baked opinion about how form and content were supposed to fit together and make meaning, I had started out writing "from my heart." So as not to contaminate my "poetic voice," I had thought it best not to read too many other poets. And in my naiveté about things literary in the publishing world, I had sent a sheaf of so-called poems to Toni Morrison, the only black editor I had heard of. I took it as a sign from the universe that although we were years apart in age, Ms. Morrison and I shared the same birthday, and added to that, the first character introduced in her novel *Song of Solomon* bore my own father's name.

Eventually, my "manuscript" found its way to Ms. Morrison. Her response—typed by a manual typewriter on tan notepaper—explained that she did not work as a poetry editor. She all but declared that mine were not actual poems, and suggested that I read more poetry. My car knew the way to the library. I made it my business to read volumes of poems and poets, whether or not they spoke to me. After all the time I had spent, if I was not yet a poet, I would uncover the differences between my writing and theirs, and hone my craft until I became one of them.

At Food for Thought that day, I jotted down the information from the flyer. Probably I had thought I needed only to continue writing "in the dark," reading whatever I read, noticing whatever I noticed. But in order for me to produce a volume of real poems, several issues had surfaced that I needed to address.

I had shared occasional pieces with well-meaning friends and family, but this private writing had no serious readers. What I needed was someone, preferably a poet, to give me useful feedback about whether the poems made sense, if indeed they were poems. And I needed more time to write.

To learn to walk, first you have to grasp the idea of falling forward. My first stumble, then, was to enter the competition. Up until then I had been reasonably satisfied with a few revised, would-be poems, but what if a real poet read them? I had the registration details, and I was willing to risk not getting into the class.

With a clear intention to jump off this cliff, I went home that day and sent my packet of poems to Carol Muske, a renowned poet and that year's workshop leader. In short order, they notified me that I was in; I would be one of the 10, writing and critiquing poems. Being accepted was one thing. Being accepted only to fail the class was a bigger risk. If that happened, I would no longer be able to convince myself that I was becoming a poet. From the first class, things were just as I had feared: I was a technologist at a literary soirée, a commoner at the royal ball. Many of the students were seasoned writers; some even awaited word of publication for manuscripts they had already submitted. In this new and subtle world of words, I was embarrassed by my ignorance. I could not speak in workshop jargon, nor did I understand how to give productive commentary. I merely pretended to see what the rest of them saw in the poems.

I had come this far—did I want this thing or not? And so one night a week, I sat among others who wanted it, too. I bought textbooks and memorized terms, went over poems again and again to tease out basic elements. After a while, some of the subtleties began to seep in. If I had learned nothing except how to critique my own work, I would have been grateful. There was much more to be had. The other students were tactful about my lack of experience, and full of praise for the things I attempted to do. Little did I know that this paltry showing was what "becoming" looks like.

Mid-semester, Carol Muske took me aside and blessed me with her opinion that I showed promise. "You ought to get into a graduate creative writing program," she said. Creative writing program? I had always thought most writers were English majors with exceptional gifts. "Maybe I will," I told her. When Carol brought in the national catalogue of graduate writing programs, I took it home and thumbed through it for integrity's sake. I knew the idea was water too deep for me to tread.

In the first place, I couldn't see how it was possible that someone with an undergraduate science degree could qualify for a graduate humanities program. And even if I could somehow pull it off, I had no time for school, no money, no hardship dire enough to get a tuition break, and no academic record sufficiently stellar to get a free ride.

Convinced it couldn't be done, I went back to writing in my bedroom and going to open readings. I couldn't see any avenue that would plant me in the middle of a writing community. Full of doubt, I let another year go by, waiting for my life.

You can have only what you can accept. Too much of the time, we make choices based on what we believe we are competent at doing. We secure jobs that suffice to bring home the paycheck with an occasional bonus. To paraphrase Thoreau, sometimes those very jobs lead to lives of quiet desperation, and we go to our graves with the song still in us. Sometimes our excellence will lead the way to careers with substantial financial gain and worthwhile achievement. The heart's desire, though, is manifested when we make choices based on our magnificence. When great possibility is hidden from your view, you have to have faith that the sun of infinite possibility is shining. It breaks through the clouds whenever you say yes.

Imagine that there are 20 or 30 people gathered to read poetry at a 19th-century gristmill alongside a creek in a natural area that runs through the middle of the city. Imagine that you can feel tradition emanating from the original heavy oak floorboards, the hand-hewn beams, the stone walls. It's an open reading, rather quiet. Very orderly. It has the feel of a bona fide poetry crowd. You sign up. You take your seat, thinking that probably you will hear arcane sentences in clever, metered stanzas; wondering why you brought your improvisational experiment to read for the first time. You sweep the audience to be sure that you know no one, and no one knows you. You're the only black.

The reading begins and, as you expected, you hear a mix of polished formal quatrains and pretty-good free verse; not many amateurs, nothing akin to anything ethnic. When your turn comes, you go to the podium and read the two poems you have brought. One of them, "Reincarnation," is the improvisational piece. It begins, "I'm coming back as a melody;/ a noble thought-feeling-emotion / will give birth to me / a clear Fitzgerald's note / in Ella's throat / a whole note trebling...." You're pleased with the decent applause you get, and you take your seat. The guy beside you scribbles something on a piece of paper and hands it to you. As you read the name "Rick" and a telephone number, he whispers something about liking your poem, and that he'd like to see it. He wants you to call him.

You don't like his seeming presumption that you will call. You're thinking *Who is this guy?* and you're not about to keep his phone number. For the rest of the evening, you try to ignore the fact that he's probably sitting there, sizing you up. When the reading is over, though, he doesn't seem to be checking you out; you quickly leave.

A couple of weeks later you get a phone call from Rick. You're thrown off a little because he gets right to the point: that you never phoned or shared your poem. You mumble some excuse, and he says, "It sounded interesting, but I'd really like to see the poem. We may want to consider it for our next edition." He gives you an address and some loose guidelines about how to submit it. As it turns out, he's Richard Peabody, editor of *Gargoyle Magazine*. Embarrassed about the obvious ego trip that had you misreading his intentions altogether, you thank him and send what will become your first published poem.

In one sense you may have found your thing, and in another sense it has found you. Like a scratching at the door, it requires that you open to it, let it in. When something chooses you, choose back. Commit and follow through. When you choose back, you give your word to yourself and to the universe. When the moment presents itself, the universe is saying, "This thing has chosen you, now are you sure?" Your entire being commits to allowing your creativity to be expressed. It means that you accept the new expression as your very own channel through which the life force will surge.

Unless we consciously accept that journeys have potholes and detours, we tend to globalize our immediate situation in a way that fits our old stories (underlying assumptions) about the way life works. Until we believe that we can, we can't. If you're straddling a fence, you'll create whatever you can believe is yours: a narrow spot, a spacious dwelling place, or a whole new continent.

And so I said, *Okay, what have I got to lose?* As far as the actual credential—a master of fine arts in creative writing—was concerned, I had thought I could take it or leave it. I saw the actual degree more as a credential than as a passport to where I wanted to go. What I coveted was the process of being immersed in study of the literary canon, and writing poems and stories that could keep me grounded in my intention to express myself as a writer. I wanted to be part of a writing community with mentors, unlimited feedback about my work, and unlimited practice to get it right. I wasn't sure that the course of study that would earn me the MFA would include the experience of community.

Rather than blindly applying to the only local university that was listed in the catalogue of writing programs, I wanted first to get a sense of the kind of student who had been admitted. I don't remember all the details of my first encounter with the director of the MFA program at American University, but you sense when you have chosen to do as the Rumi poem suggests: "...People are going back and forth across the doorsill / where the two worlds touch. / The door is round and open, / Don't go back to sleep."

The director, Myra Sklarew, was a well-known poet whom I had heard of but never met. From the first hello, "gracious" was my word for her. Instead of sitting at her desk with me on the other side, she sat in one armchair and offered me the other. Instead of the interview setup with defined roles, we chatted. I don't remember about what, but I do remember that she was alert to my comfort. The high point of our conversation, though, was about something that the two of us had in common. Here was a successful poet who had an undergraduate degree in biology. Right away she invited me to come to a poetry reading at the Library of Congress. And here was someone who would make the moment easier by responding to the poems I had brought with a poignant, "Why don't you apply and see what happens?," as if she knew something about journeys.

I did apply. I was accepted.

I had no money for tuition. At the first meeting of new graduate students, we sat around a wide conference table, introducing ourselves and relating our choice of courses for the first semester. I gave my name and explained that for this first semester, I would only pay the matriculation fee, a way of registering and having a space held for one semester. I thought that I would be able to begin classes in the January term. A minimum of six credit hours was the required course load, and I had barely the cost of three credit hours in the world. University policy dictated that graduate students were not eligible for work-study in their first semester. My best bet was to matriculate and hope to save enough to begin classes in January. When I shared that I would not be taking classes, Myra, surprised, asked, "Why not?"

I stepped over personal details and said something generic about the work-study policy. To get to the bottom line, I added something like, "Financially, it's better for me to wait until January."

"All right," Myra said, and we moved on to the next student introduction. A little later, Myra interrupted the process and suggested that we take a short break. She smiled in my direction, stood up, tall, and said gently, "Can I see you for a minute?" When we got out into the hallway she said, "Come with me."

Not knowing where we were headed, I followed her down the hall and down the stairs to an office where a plaque beside the door read "Office of the Dean." The outer office receptionist greeted Myra by name and asked whether we had an appointment. Myra said, "No, but we need to see him. This will only take a few minutes."

She introduced me to the receptionist and, without another word, promptly left me standing there. The receptionist picked up an inside line and said, "Myra Sklarew has brought someone to see you. She says it will take just a few minutes," then ushered me into to the Dean's office.

He was cordial and asked if there was a problem that needed his attention. I didn't know exactly why I was there, and what I was supposed to say, but I explained my circumstances and my intention to matriculate and begin classes in January.

Casually, he picked up the telephone. "I'm sending a graduate student over to see you. See what you can do," he said. He jotted down a name, a campus building, and room number. He handed me the slip of paper.

The door is round and open. I'm walking through.

The man in personnel informed me that they sometimes bend the rules, and that if I thought I could manage it, I could take on a teaching assistant position for the creative writing program. My stipend would cover six hours for the semester, and would automatically be paid to the university. Myra Sklarew, the director, would explain my duties.

~

The universe is for us. Life is always conspiring to bring its expression into this realm—as me and you. It is ours to commit to opening the channel.

Without commitment, that little voice will keep meddling: *Why don't you let well enough alone? Why don't you just stay in this groove of life, doing what you're good at, and do your passion-thing as a pastime? Shouldn't you wait until you feel healthier, or the kids are on their own, or your mate comes around to your way of thinking, or you have more flexibility in your work schedule? Wouldn't it be better to do this after you lose weight? Shouldn't you let it be, and it'll come back in the next lifetime, when you will be younger?*

But ask yourself if it is it all right that someone else has an identical idea, and is running with it. Is it all right to train your light to the dimmer switch?

Another passage of Goethe's quote about creativity and commitment says, "A whole stream of events issues from the decision, raising in one's favor all manner of unforeseen incidents and meetings and material assistance which no man could have dreamed would have come his way." If you've had a secret dream that you have harbored since you were 12 or since your 53rd birthday, and it has declared itself, all the chances, all the knowledge, all the resources you need are available now. You are in your right place, coming into grand readiness. Now is the time to give yourself permission to be outrageous, strange, powerful, and beautiful in your expression. Every atom of every cell knows your desire to manifest this thing. Your human self can be shored up by the spiritual nourishment. And spiritual practices put you in touch with your essential nature. Your perception can be true, your belief clear; your heart's desire can take root, bear fruit, and prosper.

You make the commitment, and personal transformation as well as a new form on the planet are foregone conclusions. You put into felt words what you wish to out-picture, and this sets in motion the energy that calls to you whatever you claim. The feeling of it will be real (say, you really are an urban gardener, growing and selling herbs to high-end restaurants). When you do so, you plant the seed in the mystery of a creative medium of the invisible Infinite.

Again, you train your mind, feelings, and emotions to believe what you want to believe: that being a wildly successful urban gardener is possible, and the world is waiting for your special tarragon and lemongrass. The truck has your logo on the side panel. Your subconscious mind will release the limited view of you as the paid employee who is building someone else's dream, and it will accept the desired replacement: you sending the delivery truck packed with fresh herbs to posh addresses.

Getting serious about creating your particular dream expression is like starting another life. Every cell is now convinced that this new thing is what the body is required to promote and support. And though your body may look the same, your cells are made new. You recycle, using your body for the next life-affirming purpose. Neural networks, hormones, hands and feet—they all turn toward this new manifestation. Acting in concert, the parts grow stronger by seeing it as already done. Still, they must do something daily that confirms that, indeed, you are engaged in consciously creating something original. The to-be herb gardener may plant seeds in a window box, and when they grow, give the herbs as gifts. Or she may take a class in accounting. Her body wants to confirm the feeling of success.

Spiritual nourishment strengthens your resolve, opening you up to see greater possibility and allowing the underlying principles of manifestation to become conscious. Maintaining a daily practice of meditation, contemplation, and affirmation shores up certainty, clarifies belief, and renders your perceptions true. The mental picture and accompanying conviction you hold of being a successful urban gardener needs all the physical trappings of productivity, all the bright smiles on the faces of satisfied clients, workers and customers. The feeling-ness is the joy of fulfillment, the freedom of individual expression.

Ripples from the smallest pebble of burgeoning creativity tossed into the pond of your life affect all things. To commit is to know that an Absolute Indescribable Infinite Great Something has the power to bring into form everything that is needed for the highest good of all concerned. The little plot of land between buildings will become a garden. All manner of herbs will love the soil, and thrive in just the right angle of sun. The gardener's business will meet with unlimited success: chefs will be grateful for fresh, local produce; and customers will flock to their restaurants.

Cultivating a Clearer Mind

In order to commit, you have to be clear about your intention, and mentally evaporate the fog that stymies your imagination. Too much of the time, we are unaware that we can take stock and change whatever it is that has us seeing only limitations. Observing whatever persists in your inner world, and observing also the situations that inspire it, will land you in the midst of more clarity, a surer focus, and an unswerving authenticity.

This doesn't mean that you have to spend every spare moment searching for beliefs in order to change them. How perfect is it that on this human plane, where our beliefs become manifest at a somewhat slowed-down pace, we have the opportunity to look at what we've co-created? At any moment you can look around at your life and see what you believe. In fact, we are hard-wired to become aware of our own beliefs. This life is set up for each of us to thin out our own forest of attitudes and perceptions. And we get plenty of opportunities—small and major—to do the work.

We can step back and consider how we get from our thoughts to our ultimate take on reality. When we accept strongly held thoughts and opinions about the way things really are, our thoughts crystallize into beliefs. Our beliefs determine our attitudes, the stances we take in life. Our attitudes become the filters through which we perceive any experience. And for each of us, perception of experience becomes reality. Seemingly automatically, the judge within directs all of this traffic.

So not only do we need to notice the traffic—the thoughts we hold—but also the narrow trails we have put in place to arrive at conclusions about life. Our conscious mind is one place where, squarely, we can observe our personal beliefs and change them to create different experiences. Take your political or religious beliefs, for example. Probably you're in touch with them. Beliefs and perceptions that are hidden from your conscious mind, however, present a different challenge.

Perception is at the crux of the matter. It can be true and clear, or it can be distorted, and chances are you won't know the difference. We live in family groups, entertain friends, and navigate through a world of cultures, all of which influence our thinking and determine the stories we internalize as reality.

Over time we all hold onto what we "have reason to believe is true." Sometimes the filter has come from values you adopt; sometimes more subtle cues have come from observing how things seem to unfold. You take on pre-judgments—prejudices—from those close to you, and the well of all of humanity's past conclusions about life and the way it all goes on.

If you wander closer to the heart of the matter, you'll find that pre-judgments have dictated which peoples have which skill sets, which gender possesses which sensibility, whether human nature is fundamentally good or bad, and countless other beliefs about life and choice. From these distorted modes of perception, we create experiences that bear out the same old views. All evidence to the contrary is filtered out. Assumed talents, abilities, skills, or lack of them are manifested, then observed as proof of "the truth." *I can't boil water. I can't carry a tune. Comedians are not serious people. Scientists don't believe in God.*

It isn't easy to remove the filters. But we have feelings and emotions that are the automatic messengers, telling us how, inside, we are responding to people and events: *I feel hurt, I am angry, I am joyful, I feel hopeful, I feel guilty.* "Positive and negative" is among the many polarities that come with the human experience. "Love and fear" is another. Some feelings we classify as positive—free, energetic, cheerful, skillful, honest, generous. When we look deeply at these feelings, we can sense the impulse of an unselfish love of all life. Negative feelings—guilty, betrayed, resentful, jealous, rejected, inadequate—we see as bad, painful. In them we see the impulse or root of fear. Most of us will attest to the fact that life-affirming feelings boost our body's ability to thrive, and negative feelings interfere with our ability to function at a peak level.

Small wonder that when we interact, we rely on our feelings to indicate that people or situations are either positive or negative. We seek to have fewer painful experiences, and, in the attempt to rid ourselves of them, we fight, avoid, or otherwise resist people or situations where the potential for painful interaction is high. In actuality it is the bad feeling that we wish to escape. On some level we know that these feelings signify roadblocks to the expression of our real self.

Thinking that something outside our selves causes us to feel as we do is flawed thinking. It is actually our beliefs that generate feelings. Because of a belief we may misinterpret not only what seems to be occurring, but also our response to it. In order to flee from, fight, or resist the bad feeling, we react to the "out-there" person or situation in a way that we believe will quell our upset-ness. We see our reaction as a corrective measure. Unwittingly, we remain powerless before situations, believing that something outside of our selves has power over us.

The good news is that emotion itself can be a benevolent blinking light, announcing a point of choice, an opportunity to change a belief that underlies a feeling. Feelings can signal that something is out of sync with the reality that the inner knower knows. If you feel hurt and rejected because you didn't get that phone call you were hoping for, you may be thinking that you are not being valued, based on your identification with your own belief that you are not valuable. The inner knower knows that you are valuable regardless of what anyone thinks, or says, or does, and no matter what you, yourself, think, say, or do. In such a situation, you are out of sync with the deeper truth. And beliefs can wreak havoc on your peace of mind even when other people are not involved. You can be just walking along, minding your business, and guilt can slap you sober because you're harboring a "should" or "should not" which has laid down rules for your life. You globalize the smallest mistake and pretty soon you're in the spiral of personal failure that can bring on a bout of hopelessness. You constantly calculate your worth based on comparisons to other people, better and worse. "What if" can scare you into avoidance of the very expression you long for. This is about the unconscious patterns that put us out of touch with ourselves, and leave us confused and suffering.

In your car, when the "check engine" light begins to blink, you don't smash the indicator light or run away from it. You see it for what it is, a warning that something is out of line. And aren't you relieved that it works and you won't be suddenly stranded. You take the car in for a check.

We don't have to walk around feeling powerless or angry or rejected. We don't have to fight others or defend against life for fear of suffering. Clearing out mind clutter makes more space for expression of our real selves.

Acceptance—as a transformative response to life in general, and emotions in particular—is a useful tool to move this process along. As a response to an emotion, acceptance can be a challenging concept to grasp. Letting feelings be feelings, rather than thinking that feelings are facts, can bring you to the present moment. Bringing Presence to the moment, or bringing yourself into the "now" moment, is where all the power lies, and where nothing else can prevail. Though an emotion may be triggered by something you heard or saw, that Presence response has indicated not a fact, but a hidden belief, that is inside the sphere that is you.

Realizing this, you can let go of the emotion—not the situation, but the sadness, or the feeling of powerlessness or inadequacy. And you can turn your attention to the belief you hold. Perhaps you believe that a violation has occurred because someone has an opposing opinion, or perhaps you think that you are lacking in some way, or not valuable.

Here is the clearing-out moment where you replace the flawed belief with the truth. Here is the opportunity for more freedom, more peace, and more expression of who you really are.

The replacement truth is always a life-affirming belief that opposes the limited view. When you get that jolt of realization that you are a terrific expression in this world, that you are no less than the trees and the stars, valuable because you spring from the most high—you're home, safe, beyond reproach. You are a power center unto yourself, not subject to anyone or anything outside of yourself. When you accept your state of mind for what it is, you can change it and choose your state of being.

Clearing-out Exercises

1. Take every opportunity to use this simple, mind-clearing process as you allow more focused energy to flow toward your commitment. For example, say somebody "disses" you, says something that you consider disrespectful, puts you down. You feel sad or wounded. Embarrassment or anger kicks in. You push back with words or body language, or you withdraw and nurse your wounds. Take the following steps:

- Notice the feeling (hurt) that comes up and note the emotion (anger) with which you respond. The feeling/emotion is your signal.

- Accept the feelings for what they are. Like the weather, they are neither good nor bad. They are just feelings, not facts about who you are. In accepting them, you become the observer of your mind, breaking your identification with them.

- Recognize that an assumption is at work, generating the feeling. It is an assumption you have made about your value or worth, or about life. Perhaps you never knew that you held a belief about being less than terrific. Your feeling and emotion are generated by the belief you hold about yourself.

- Replace that belief. Use your sanctuary statement. Change that assumption. Once you replace the error-belief with the essential truth of who you are, the "bad" feeling will not come up, the emotion will not be generated, and you will live more at peace. Anyone can intend ill will in a word, but if you do not identify with it, it will not penetrate the unassailable truth of who you are.

2. In your journal, list at least one hidden assumption (or as many as you like) that may be limiting you—one that you are conscious of, or one that you suspect is beyond your awareness. Let it be specific to what you can and cannot do, or what someone like you should or should not do as it regards

creative expression. Consider a life-affirming replacement for the limiting belief.

3. Adopt the habit of fighting nothing smaller than you are. Do not resist your "negatives"/demons/dragons. Find any support you need in order to change focus. Clear out. The only power of these demons is the power that you give to them.

4. If you have identified even the faintest inkling of the creative expression your heart desires, then commit to it. Don't worry about turning back. Don't play the what-if game with yourself.

Think of where you are going. What stands in your way? In your journal, make a list of obstacles as you imagine them now. Then, one by one, write a brief and earnest comment about how each potential obstacle is really a brilliant opportunity.

5. Create an affirmation about commitment to develop your chosen creative expression. Examples:

Every day in every way I grow in receptivity, courage, and acceptance.

In gratitude, I accept that this expression is already mine.

Affirm your commitment to maintaining a spiritual foundation. Examples:

My thoughts, words, and activities are grounded in the truth of my being.

I am whole and complete just as I am.

6. Create a physical space where your new expression will be developed. Claim a room in your house or a corner in your room as the place reserved exclusively for such development. Stamp it with your identity—add personal touches that ex-

press your intention. Furnish it with all the special bells and whistles that bring it alive for you: pens, cutlery, earphones, microscope, mirrors. Devote a realistic period of time each day, and spend it on the inner and outer work of bringing your "thing" into the world. Announce your intention to have no distractions as you work in that time and space—a do-not-disturb message.

7. Surround yourself with clever reminders: a miniature truck with your initials painted on the side can represent your delivery service; miniature tap-dance slippers hung from a coat hook or a miniature saxophone bracelet charm will brighten an uninspired morning; a desk plate displaying your name on the windowsill or actual business card in a holder on your bedroom dresser are concrete promises.

8. Create a ritual to mark this time of planting your idea in the infinite creative medium. Include objects that symbolize ideas becoming things. An example: in a flowerpot, plant actual fast-growing grass seeds and watch the shoots come up. Put the flowerpot on a window sill or in a spot easily within your field of vision. Care for the grass, and when it becomes necessary, add it to your lawn. Then begin again.

Nothing is work unless you'd rather be doing something else.
—George Halas

6
DIVING INTO DEEP KNOWLEDGE
AND PRACTICE

O nce I began studies in a writing program, I understood
that a sure way to gain knowledge about the thing you
want to do is to dive, step-by-leap, into it. It's a new reality.
Once you immerse yourself in the culture of it, you live in a
country where you may be familiar with the language, but
now you start noticing the idioms and dialects, the innuendos
and silences.

Knowledge evolves. You're hungry for the totality of all the
facts, ideas and understanding from experts over centuries
and from today's research in every conceivable medium. For
instance, I waded through Middle English, and fixated on
modern form. Contemporary luminaries had me considering
what I might add to the conversation. I mimicked and studied
voices and styles and ways to make meaning in more poems,

short stories, and essays than I thought possible. I was awed by much of what I encountered in the literature, and even by the writing of some of my fellow students. Imitation as an exercise pushed me more deeply into my own expression.

It doesn't matter if you find plenty of what might look like competition. The idea that you have to be born with talent is overrated. Staying the course is all. We're all potential geniuses and it has little to do with IQ. Anyone bent on developing their heart's desire gets in touch with extraordinary aptitude or an exceptional inclination in creative power.

You gain knowledge and experience, and your senses begin to report deeper resonance. No longer hidden from you, signs of beauty tell you more than your rational mind can figure. These are creativity perks, the moments of solitude when wonderment falls into your lap.

For the two years of graduate school, I had opted to moonlight in the lab each weekend, four double shifts—evening and night—for full-time pay. One midnight, instead of a double shift I had done a single, and was grateful to be headed home.

At home my children would be asleep, and I anticipated the sitter leaving, giving me quiet time. Contrary to what I had once thought, after-lab nights were my best times for writing. By then I had exhausted my ability to focus on computations and procedures; my right brain would be ready to take over from my left brain's perfect discipline. The mere idea of playing in the language of poetry made me eager to close all doors except the one that opened to my dream.

As I drove through the city streets, I'm sure I did what I usually did in the car—work the "as if" idea by picking up where I had left off many hours before, imagining the book of poems that would deliver me.

Probably my mind went to the same hope—that someday I would be able to call myself a real writer. Along with my course work, it seemed that I struggled with every single line of the poems I wrote for workshop each week. The solid master's thesis that I was attempting to create would become the foundation of my first book. Some people wrote for the workshop. I wrote for the out-there editor who would read my manuscript.

When I pictured myself, I was always on a stage, reading from my book, which always had a blue cover. I knew that when the day came, I would explain my attempt to incorporate the spirit of improvisation; how the trope of virtuoso listing conveys the flatted-fifth of jazz. Something to dazzle. Sometimes I imagined reading my most serious piece, a poem about the murder of Emmett Till with its slant rhyme intended to convey the loss of childhood innocence. In fantasy, I always paused for effect, allowing the phrase "blood on snow" to linger. And then, as if to let the audience breathe, I would switch to my first published poem, the one with scat-bop rhythm, more style than substance. I had no trouble hearing the fantasy audience erupting in applause; then, without looking up, me saying "thank you" and closing my book. I had rehearsed that scenario until it played in my head like a movie.

Driving home with my reverie, I swam in gratitude for the expression I had found. If I continued, day after day, to do my inner work and be present with that movie, to feel—the way I felt some nights when I had written a good line or paragraph—that words would continue to come, my imagination would not fail me. I had come through high water before I had known that I could swim.

The way we frame our experience is completely within our own control. When we choose gratitude as the lens through which we see things, vision improves. And with that, any part of any creative expression improves. When you are more open to noticing what is awesome in your ordinary life, it changes your experience of would-be mundane tasks you wish you could avoid.

I never took any successes for granted. Sometimes upsetting thoughts would crash in on my contentment scenarios. That night, I probably had my usual concern about any detail that might doom a piece that I had been working on, like tone and mood in a persona poem I wanted to finish. It was a poem that might have turned into a story about Jesse, a man who had made the local headlines as the first homeless person to freeze to death that year. (Even though poems were my only language, I entertained ideas for short stories.) When you're engaging in stream-of-consciousness thinking, you can jump directly from a family secret to a metaphor, and from that to syntax or structure or revising any missteps. You can dwell on poetic rhythm, timing, and flow and suddenly be into the universe and the rhythm of cycles and changes and your life and the kids' lives and whether or not you should stop for orange juice at the 7-Eleven, and character-driven stories, and the title for the sonnet you have written, or the essay about writer's block, or the three-line envoy of your sestina that isn't working, and what would happen if your thesis committee throws it out. After all, your thesis has only 21 poems, not enough for a book.

Fear of failure can sometimes be a thief, one thought away. You remember the panic about the C+ you got the first year, on your first Chaucer exam. You and Middle English. You and the professor with an issue.

It was always your choice to sit in the front row of any class; you have fewer distractions to deal with, and you don't miss a word that tumbles out of the professor's mouth. Even so, you can miss cues and signs in body language that can trip you up.

In fleeting moments, you have wondered about the professor. He never calls on you. He seems to prefer to hold court with the scholars, and you are a writer. And so one day, when the professor says he'd like to have a word and asks you to wait after class, trouble rumbles in your ears.

He leans back on his desk in front of where you sit, crosses his arms, and asks something like, "Why are you studying Chaucer?"

You could go for the short answer about your preference among requisite courses, but you fumble an answer about the canon and the gap that you want to close in your own knowledge, the evolution of literary excellence, et cetera.

"From what I have observed," he continues, "you are not particularly interested in my course."

What can you say? You have plunged into the complexities of Chaucer's *The Canterbury Tales* with all you can muster, and you think you have begun to grasp a perspective of the long scheme of literature. You know the first exam is coming.

"I notice," the professor goes on, "that you are the first to close your books when the class is over, and the first one out the door. You sit in the front row, and I find it disrespectful." He suggests that if you're not interested, you could at least sit elsewhere.

You read the code before he can finish his last sentence. His reading of your haste to get to your responsibilities in the office or at home is that you couldn't care less about a subject that—it is hoped—he loves, and by inference, you couldn't care less about his power in your life. If this is the only place where he can find fuel for his animosity, you had better head him off at the pass. And so, apologetically, you tell him that he's mistaken. The truth is that you are unaware of rushing, but your schedule is tight.

But he isn't finished. He starts making conversation.

"You are in the writing program; what do you plan to do?" he asks.

You tell him that eventually you want to publish, and put writing in the center of your life. You tell him that you love language and ideas, and that poetry can get at both in a way no other form can.

Then he launches his guided missile, "It's too late for you, you know," he says. "Writers don't wait until they're 40 to get started. You're up against young minds who have studied literature for years. The likes of…" and he names a brilliant younger poet who teaches in the department, "is what you're up against. He published his first book in his twenties."

But I was way ahead of him. "I know," I said, and in so many words I told him what was true: that even if I never published, I loved to write and I would continue writing. It felt like what I was meant to do. Until I was in the program, I had never understood how scholarship would inform the whole process for me.

When I walked slowly out of the room that day, I vowed that he would not deter me. I was not sure what his prejudice was about, but I sloughed off the idea that I could ever be bothered by anyone else's mistaken view of my dream.

A little later when I took the first exam, I thought I had done okay. But when I opened the blue book to the back page and saw the red "C+," I nearly panicked. As long as my grade affected my future in the program, I would be at risk. I believed that he needed to flaunt his low opinion of who I was, and prove to me that he had power in my life. From him, I needed only the grade that I deserved. You cannot change another person. But you can stand in your own power and let him be. If his idea of respect was my idea of soothing his ego, no problem.

From that day forward, for the rest of the semester, I approached him as if he were the smartest person I had ever met. When I went over the first exam with him, it was not to convince him that his marks were blatantly unfair—though I believed that they were—but to convince him that I could be further illumined with his brilliance. Many an hour I sat in his office, ostensibly to clarify details in my notes, and while I was at it, double down on questions that might show up on future exams. I listened while he spouted his small opinions about his colleagues, the new literary voices, the culture. I found him to be a bitter man who, I believed, would perish in a dungeon of his own making.

You never know who may not want your dream to happen, but so what? You make your front-row seat into the model of attentiveness, and always, after class, you leisurely meander in the direction of the door. You make sure to keep your whole being trained on what you really want and ignore any provocation from the sidelines. A- was my final grade for the course. At the end of my first year, on the recommendation of the department faculty, I received a graduate honor award that would come sufficiently close to covering my tuition for the remainder of my studies.

The universe is always for us. In the development of your expression, you dive into the unknown, which can reveal remarkable synchronicities. Course by course, you acquire strategic knowledge. Moment by year, you give yourself over to practice modes that will take you there. It's how you allow you dream to happen.

Going home from the lab that night, I drove along the east side of the city. Just before crossing the bridge over the Anacostia River, there was a stretch of roadway where you could glimpse nearly the entire southeast section of the city.

Right there, the giving-ness of the universe was about to seize my inattention and deliver more than I could imagine. The land near the river had a flat horizon, and at night it was black as pitch. That particular night, a blue-black, moonless sky provided barely enough contrast to make the land-edge visible.

As I veered into that stretch of roadway, I saw it: a golden, odd-angled, half-moon had slipped through the slit between earth and sky, and was now floating upward—a natural wonder. I pulled over to take it in. As I idled on the shoulder of the road, I fumbled in my purse for my notebook, then jotted down these words: *I can see half the moon rising late, hanging off kilter, loitering, as if the other half could catch up.* Out of nowhere, at any time, a spectacular sighting of nature doing her thing can lift you and change your mood to optimism.

I could not have known then, that in a distant-future time, I would struggle with the ending of an important poem about the cost of trying to do it all, have it all. I would go to my crate-file of loose-leaf pages where, over years, I would have scribbled images and scraps of poems. I would come upon that night's scribbling—the lines delivered by the universe, and they would be the perfect ending for my poem. Nothing can match the flow of giving-ness from the Infinite.

That night, however, I sat for as long as I pleased, taking it all in, then pulled back onto the roadway and headed home, simply grateful for the beauty of a moonrise.

&

Immersing yourself in the culture of the expression you're moving toward will change the vibrational frequency of where you are now to that of where you are going. Everything in the universe, visible and invisible, is energy, vibrating filaments of energy. All energy—from the densest forms, to what we loosely describe as space—has a vibrational frequency, a specific rate at which the atoms, sub-atomic particles, and smaller elements are in constant motion. Some frequencies we classify as solid, some as gases, some as visible, some as invisible. Think about sound waves, light waves. Thought, too, is energy. We experience some vibrational frequencies with our senses. Our skin, eyes, nose, ears, tongue—all are interpreters of frequencies common to us all: consider an encounter with a rotten egg, rough pavement under bare feet, the blinding flash of a camera.

In the Foreword to Penney Pierce's *Frequency: The Power of Personal Vibration*, Michael Beckwith writes, "The world's scientific communities agree that energy comprises all things, and that energy systems are conscious...So when we are dealing with the subject of energetic frequencies, it is not a mysterious 'something' out in the stratosphere, but directly in our inner spaces." Energy in the form of belief, thought, feeling and emotion, too, has a particular vibrational signature. The frequency at which our cells vibrate contributes to the overall frequency of our individual energetic field.

As a simplified interpretation, consider that the beliefs, thoughts, feelings, and emotions that give rise to all experience come together first in various energetic configurations that are frequency-specific. We have the ability to experience those vibrational configurations of our own beliefs and emotions as our personal feeling-ness, a certain quality to our awareness of them.

In our daily lives, we try on feelings that we have built around all kinds of experience, and allow the tried-on feeling-ness—pleasant, unpleasant—to determine whether or not we might enjoy something previously unknown to us.

The way that we each view the world, and the way we relate to our views, is unique. We are attracted to corresponding frequencies everywhere in our environment. Barring any circumstance that might intervene, our frequency becomes our personal atmosphere.

Innate in us, too, is the capacity to be in sync with the frequency of any outcome we desire, thereby manifesting that outcome as the atmosphere in which we operate. The potential reality where our creative expression flourishes is also frequency specific; it has a certain vibration in potential. Once we shift our vibration to that frequency, we are aligned with it; we become one with it.

In order to make that leap, you have to live in that mindset for some part of every day. Maintain a single focus on what you want to do. Be present with the feeling of being in the life where you are that thing, have that thing, do that thing.

The hours I spent in my car, running that movie where I was on stage reading from my book of poems, were hours that I was no longer in the frequency of my time-bound everyday life. When you dwell in a feeling-ness that is outside of time and space, you are there.

Begin to build the habits of the furniture designer that you are becoming. At this time you ignore the dictates of the mar-ketplace—the earning power, the tendency to conform to consumer tastes or critics' praise. This is the moment to seize on knowledge having to do with properties of various woods; learn about proportions and scale. In your imagination, shape what you hear and see to coincide with your dream of com-fortable contours for the human body; this is your creative intelligence. To a craftsperson, beauty and function inform every decision. Train your eye to see deeply, and, like a child, sense the essence of things. Reshape your conception of an item's accustomed use to the beauty and function you desire.

Occasionally someone finds she has vaulted into the un-known overnight, and brought a magnificent expression into existence. Sometimes the gestation period is long. So be it.

Allow as long as it takes to be synchronized to the frequency at which you vibrate with your highest expression. Along the way you will receive your message in a dream. Your Myra Sklarew, your poetry reading, your unexpected income, perfect timing, and organization of every detail necessary to deliver the fullness of your singular gift—all of that will appear. If your heart's desire is to create an institution or program, see yourself at the head, grateful for all the lives you have touched. Give the dancer inside you full reign, and the dancer will instruct every atom of your being to pirouette.

Knowledge

As far as acquiring knowledge is concerned, school worked for me, but one size doesn't fit all. Traditionally we have trained ourselves to accept information and understanding that comes from outside of us. While clearly valuable, traditional paths of pursuing knowledge can set up barriers to other ways of knowing.

Direct, intuitive knowledge is especially associated with creative expression. Outside of the usual "book learning," insights, hints, and nudges are natural triggers that engage your imagination. Imagination attracts direct comprehension of any subject.

As a student, I was always trying to tease out abstract ideas. I once spent months trying to perfect a poem that dealt with the concept of hypocrisy—condemning others for their behavior when yours is even worse. For originality, I thought to modernize the chauvinistic biblical story of the Pharisees. I decided to challenge myself and use a fixed form to convey the blind complexity of hypocrisy.

I labored with a sestina, a complex, thirty-nine-line poem with six stanzas of six lines each, which repeat the end words of the lines of the first stanza, only in different order. The sestina form ends with a three-line envoy using the six words again. Talk about a labyrinth. And I started out using biblical language in a biblical setting.

Off and on for what seemed like ages, I worked on drafts. No matter what I tried, I continued to run into the need for concrete elements that would make it fresh and original, yet keep to the crux of the matter that was so clear in the parable.

For hours one night I sat writing paragraphs explaining the poem to myself; I had pages of drafts strewn all over the bed. Yet I was unable to make the subject fit the form that I insisted it should have.

Finally I gave up. I collected the papers, stacked them together, tossed them beside the bed, fell back on my pillow, and flicked off the light.

Before I could settle toward sleep, a voice came clear with a story to tell. *In the first place, don't mess with no Pharisee men. They don't mind taking your time, but they treat you back-street.* No biblical language, no meter, no holy temple. I flicked on the light, grabbed my yellow pad, and began writing. The poem ended up being a dramatic monologue in the voice of the biblical woman who was about to be stoned to death by the Pharisees. These were the people who slinked away when Jesus implored that any one of them beyond reproach should throw the first stone. A sestina could never convey what this woman had to say. My takeaway for the umpteenth time was that form and content go together to make meaning. Never force the issue. Let intuition bring in the knowledge.

Obviously, in order to become a successful classical pianist, you must know unequivocally how to read and perform classical music on the piano. Living in the vibration of a classical pianist means that your mind and your fingers have knowledge of a classical repertoire; you are familiar with the habits and lives of the masters. You become absorbed in all kinds of esoteric elements other people ignore, things like quirks in composers and their compositions. Still, when you sit on that bench, the music is delivered uniquely through you.

Using ingenuity and imagination, an inventor produces a completely original thing, because she can see beyond what is known. Still, most inventors have a fundamental grasp of dynamic laws and principles in related fields. The studies of technology, physics, and design are examples. Remaining open and receptive to all forms of knowledge fertilizes the flower of your expression. As you are in touch with your inner spirit, you come into intuitive knowing.

Opinions and instructions from well-meaning others can be seductive. Our loved ones and teachers want the best for us, sometimes according to their own ideas of what is best. They may not know the unique you that wants to do amazing things. They can share advice and you can listen with a keen ear for what serves you, and leave the rest. We are individuals running on this life track, which is not unlike the circular track of a sports field, each one of us in our own lane in the spiral of our own evolution. Whenever we stand in our own power and give ourselves permission to dream, choose, and create our heart's desire, we are in the right lane.

Practice

Once you commit, passion sustains your motivation to continue. All of your physiology—including your brain's neural networks—gets into the act, perfecting that way of being in the world.

Bogus ideas about talent can sabotage the process. One school of thought about talent says it is innate, and another says that we come into life with the capacity to express in any way we choose. Although talent may look or feel predestined, most researchers who study such things agree that talent is developed, not born.

In *The Talent Code*, Daniel Coyle underscores the importance of deliberate, methodical development of a chosen expression. He sees the talent code as key to unlocking the neurology of how we become good at what we love doing. He quotes Dr. George Bartzokis, a UCLA neurologist and myelin researcher, who puts it succinctly: "All skill, all language, all music, all movements are made of living circuits, and all circuits grow according to certain rules." Coyle goes on to explain how and why myelin—a lipoprotein that forms a sheath around certain nerve fibers in our brain—is the "holy grail of acquiring skill." This sheath becomes an insulator, so that electrical signals traveling through a neural circuit cannot leak out. The signal, then, becomes stronger, faster.

With every thought, movement, or feeling, we send an electrical impulse through a chain of nerve fibers. It's called firing a circuit. When we fire our circuits, myelin forms a sheath of insulation, adding new layers each time. Whenever errors force us to slow down and correct them, we add more layers of myelin. The more myelin, the more speed and accuracy. The more speed and accuracy, the more graceful the skill. In this way, every human skill is developed.

With such a model, you can see why it is important to think, act, and feel—to practice—in ways that generate the most productive signals through your circuits.

Coyle calls it "deep practice," and in it we operate at the edges of our ability; we make mistakes. Rather than simply courting failure, we experience missed-takes that get us to struggle and stretch to overcome the difficulty, and this generates a thicker myelin sheath, making us quicker, wiser, more skilled.

My graduate studies included a semester living with every conceivable fixed form of verse, and I was required to create a formal piece of my own each week. I practiced marrying subject to meter and rhyme in sonnets, in villanelles, in everything from limerick and rondeau to elegy, ode, and then some. Shifting gears, I had to find my own combinations of blank verse, free verse, narrative, lyrical, prose poems—whatever worked best for what I was trying to convey.

Over an engaging semester of literary translation, I translated much of the well-known epic poem "Song of Lawino," by Ugandan poet Okot p'Bitek, from his native Acholi to English. It meant finding a native speaker who was local, and finding an Acholi translation dictionary, though a Luo dictionary was the closest thing available. It meant keeping the poetic integrity of the original work.

"The best words in the best order." This was a working definition of poetry famously given by Coleridge. Trying to get it right each week for two years was invaluable practice for finding the best words and setting them down in the best order.

And so we break the talent code by practicing strategically. Repetition is crucial. Forming new pathways in our brains and sheathing those circuits require that we stretch to get it right, over and over again. It's like placing your feet, step-together-step, deliberately, repeatedly, until you learn the steps of an intricate dance.

You can see how this resonates with wisdom teachings about turning thought into experience, such as Biblical, Kabbalistic, and Upanishadic laws about sowing and reaping (cause and effect). Whatever beliefs and feelings you hold in mind will show up as your experience. The principle is always working, and seems to be more obvious to us when we are creating something desirable. Technique is great, but ultimately the practice must be a feeling thing. The feeling of reaching again and again grows the skill in us. We grow by trying to grow. How perfect is that?

If you know that you have to make errors in order to get good at what you want, then you can include making errors as part of the plan. You say to yourself, *This is how my body follows the dictates of my mind. This is how it looks when I am at this stage of being a great choreographer.* And once you are dancing, it feels natural, and you forget all of the stumbles that got you there.

Practice. Play the part. If videographer is what you really are, you will find the places where people do this, and hang out there. Call a small group together and share your amateur footage with them to experience the sheer courage of moving it out of your garage—no longer keeping it a secret, and no longer pretending that it does not matter to you.

As you develop the outlet for your creativity, your inner work is vital for harmonizing your frequency with that of your gift. And your outer work engages your physical body with purposeful activity, from the discovery stage, to commitment, and on through the trial-and-error stages of knowledge and practice. Imagine that you are writing the development of your creative expression as a novel. Each chapter covers an important plot point or action point designed to advance your story-of-becoming in a significant way. You may be aware of some actions you need to take to complete your novel, but in this dynamic process you are probably unaware of all of the steps that will get you to your personal arrival scene. You can, however, be alert to them as they come up, and, diligently, you can execute them.

How will you know that you are on the right road? As you pass through those action points, your heart will leap with the joy of recognition. You will be renewed and inspired as you celebrate each small completion, each sign post that informs you that this is the road.

How will you know for sure that you have arrived? At the end of all the best stories, the author doesn't merely tell you what happens; you don't read, "And then she found her long-lost sister." Instead, the writer shows you. You get the description of a city marketplace where the fragrance of lilies emanates from a stall; the author captures the scene with its handmade jewelry and vibrant silk scarves; you can almost hear the clamor of merchants and customers bartering wares. The protagonist notices the back of a woman's head, how it is tilted the way her sister used to tilt hers whenever she had a question; notices a familiar hand stroking the fold of a shawl. And when the head turns at just the right angle to expose the woman's profile...et cetera, et cetera.

Imagine that at the end of a story about the development of a longed-for career, the author writes, simply, "And now she is a successful rabbi."

It won't do. We want the real scene—setting, action, dialogue—that shows that she has arrived. Such a scene would have the rabbi in an impressive synagogue with its terra cotta, cathedral-style dome crowned with a bronze Star of David. Stained-glass rose windows would stream brilliant sunlight into the sanctuary. She would be standing at the platform from which the Torah is read, framed by twin brass menorahs and with the Eternal Light hanging over the Holy Ark from a gold-leaf ceiling. And in her most sonorous voice, she would give a great sermon to an overfull congregation.

Now imagine the scene where you, yourself, have become the embodiment of what you always intended to be. Focus on all the elements that are required for you to know and feel that you have arrived.

As you allow all the images to come up, you can use all the senses and bring in all possible detail of yourself engaged in your creative gift. And you keep this picture before you, within you. When, in real time, you find yourself in that scene or an even better one, you will know that you have arrived: you have consciously manifested a new creative expression.

All of the parts come together. You begin with that dramatic scene and, as clearly as possible, work back to the present moment. Say you are becoming a master chef, and your arrival scene has you glancing up from the counter in the television studio kitchen, smiling into the camera as you demonstrate for a million viewers the simplicity of preparing perfect apple-walnut fitters served with your version of crème anglaise. Working back to the present moment, your outer work may be to go online and research the credentials of a master chef, or to Williams-Sonoma to shop for your first food processor, or to phone your aunt for your grandmother's recipe.

Uncover the first step that you must take in order to open your first chapter, no matter how small or mundane. Don't be distracted by all that you can't yet imagine; just know that your arrival scene is a concrete reality. Bit by bit, things coalesce into steps that, when taken, add up to progress that might seem magical. Today is day one, the first day that you are consciously in the process of becoming what your heart desires. Know that you are guided to your ultimate scene. The universe is handling everything else.

At this juncture, gratitude need not be limited to what you receive or remember receiving. Giving thanks in advance of the appearance of something you want is transformative because it assumes deep conviction that that something is already yours. Your desired end is assured of fulfillment. Even when you merely mouth the words, "I am so grateful now

that I have X," it gives you the sense that you are in the vibration of something already done.

And give thanks for the inner shifts that prove illuminat-
ing, even when outer circumstances appear to stagnate. Be
thankful for inspirations, the small daily ones that come in
the face of all that may appear as your experience, including fear, failure, false starts, and disappointment. Inspiration
keeps the hunger fed in little bits.

Do your daily study, activity, practice, testing, and training. Build the habits of the mountain climber or therapist
you are becoming. Notice the changes and celebrate the small
indications that something is beginning to move.

Cultivating an Appetite for Knowledge and Practice

The conventional faith-vs.-work idea—faith that is embodied in the way we conduct our lives—comes into play as you
engage your physicality, your hands and feet, your senses,
noticing where you go, the associations you choose. You'll
find that your busyness illuminates your inner life in curi-
ous ways.

The more you do, the hungrier you are for what is yours to
do: studying, learning, practicing, testing, pretending, training your body and mind to the new life. Take any or all of
the following suggestions as guideposts:

1. Research local classes, courses, and programs for gaining
the knowledge suited to your intention, and register for one.
Lifelong learning programs abound at local universities and
community centers.

2. Follow your imagination, and with a bold action, consider
at least three possibilities for exposure and commit to one.

For example:

- If you want to immerse your energy in physical cosmology, and Neil deGrasse Tyson is the only astrophysicist you have ever heard of, go to his website and make contact.
- Subscribe to a niche magazine like *Wine Business Monthly* that caters to the community of vintners, your to-be peers.
- Get on the mailing lists for the *Wiley-Blackwell Library Newsletter*, which delivers up-to-date information for anyone desiring to be a librarian.

3. Immerse yourself in the culture where your chosen expression thrives:

- Visit an actual shop, office, studio, arena, farm, hall, retreat, etc., where your chosen form of expression holds sway.
- Fill in your calendar with at least two related events each month.
- Engage with at least two people who are doing what you intend to do.
- Choose a mentor who is willing to share experience and expertise with you, and commit to a work schedule.

4. Create a vision board: a concrete, visual out-picturing of your completed gift with all the embellishments and details. Use your senses. Combine elements of sight, smell, sound, taste, and touch to bring it to life. Draw pictures, cut them from magazines, or visit websites for images that represent your successful manifestation. Post the collage where you can easily encounter it daily: on a bedroom wall, inside a clothes closet, on a bathroom door.

5. Spend 20 minutes each day seeing yourself as already arrived. Enter the feeling-ness. As with the mental picture that you may have developed earlier, for each step and each phase of your development, work from that scene back to the present moment. Your direction will be clear.

6. Pick and develop the most productive habits:

> ~ **Begin with time and place.** If your brain typically turns to mush at 9:00 p.m., don't look to have a brilliant creative flash at 9:30 p.m., and don't put off having creative expression time until everyone is asleep unless, of course, a sleeping house is your most productive setting.

> ~ **Consume only what nourishes you.** To be inspired, visit places that hold your idea of beauty, read and contemplate the writings that bring good tidings, study the manuals of those who succeeded, contemplate the principles that underlie success.

> ~ **Allow for the gestation process.** If need be, watch the wallpaper dry; do a no-brain thing as you wait for dream ideas to come, develop, and bear fruit.

> ~ **Focus.** You will draw all manner of things to yourself.

7. Affirm the full realization of a step in the development, or the entire enterprise of your creative gift. For example:

> *I find the perfect mannequin for my studio.*

> *I am grateful now that I have clarity, I am focused, and I release any sense of confusion.*

> *In gratitude, I express my magnificence in thought, word, and action.*

Grapes want to turn into wine.
—Rumi

7

LANDING IN CELEBRATION
AND GRATITUDE

Life does not happen to us. We do not stumble, unfocused, into what we become. Giving-ness is ever pouring out for us, and we accept it by making a conscious decision, holding a clear intention, and remaining resolute. With every fiber of my being, I wanted a published book as evidence of my intention to be a writer. No, I don't believe I ever thought "I need evidence," but the sum total of having a book would feel like a wonderful completion. I liked imagining the scene: me at the podium, the book cover, the rapt audience. In a way, making poems and stories had been like a return to childhood, when I had played movie star in crepe paper costumes at dusk in the backyard. I could work on a line or a sentence and not know that hours were passing. I could be caught up in teasing out a metaphor and miss my stop on the Metro.

One day, you find yourself in a familiar scene. How humbling it is to see your own hands, feel your own heart, hear your own voice engaged in this incomparable way. Through your sensibility, you have brought into existence a unique channel of expression for Life. By whatever name, the well of creativity remains an amazing thing.

The year after I received my MFA, while I was still working in the clinical laboratory, I had continued to publish poems in a number of literary magazines, and peddle my poetry manuscript at small presses. Now mine was frequently among the names on the schedule of venues for local poetry readings. Washington Writers Publishing House, a writing collective, turned down my manuscript that year, but gave me sufficient feedback that by the next submission date, I had revised and expanded it. Each year they published only two volumes of poetry. That next year, they published mine, and a new book by Myra Sklarew.

I stood at the podium before an audience in the auditorium of the Corcoran Gallery of Art, preparing to read a few poems from *Coping With Gravity*, my newly published volume. I can see myself, contemplating the significance of the book's design: a blue sky with a full moon rising on the cover. The first piece I read was a poem called "Moonlighting," about slaving away on the night shift. One of the passages talked about how "…a whole life costs…," especially when you are a single parent. The poem ends, "As I turn into the winding shadow of my street, I can see half the moon, rising late, loitering, as if the other half could catch up."

I marveled at how things come together, at that image so strikingly given to me years before and planted unconsciously. I remarked upon how memory and imagination can sometimes be inseparable. Aloud at the podium, I laid to rest the idea that the creation of a poem, a book—anything—is subject to rational order. That night at the Corcoran, I knew that I was no longer waiting for my life.

I like to think it was at that moment, too, that I began to jettison the tired story of my empowerment in order to try on the new identity that laid to rest the facts of survivorhood and went directly to making good. Tall order, but if you take up residence and internalize a life-so-far story based on surviving the odds, or if you really believe that the moral high ground is a free pass to any kind of deliverance, you can easily risk settling for less than the promised land. Mind, body, and spirit are always seeking to be in sync. Of course, that means that you have to begin releasing whatever you gave power to in the past that is messing with your life in the present. It's called forgiveness. I don't think I was ready for dramatic change in that department yet. When you don't know, you do what you do with what little you know and try not to sabotage your efforts to pull all your time and energy fully into the present.

Momentum isn't everything, but it's high on the list of contributing factors when you're coming into a bigger life. In the vernacular of the sacred, it's called acceptance of what comes. Second to publication, my greatest wish had been to have more time to write. In the middle of the summer, one of my contacts at AU phoned to say that their sections for creative writing were already filled, they were adding more sections, and, if I was interested, I should apply for one of the new adjunct teaching positions. I wasn't sure how that would serve me. I had not considered teaching; I knew that I could do it, but it was not my forte. I wanted a job that paid enough for me to work only four days a week and write in every minute of my off time. I figured that kind of job had to be in somebody's laboratory. Adjunct pay wouldn't begin to come close.

Still and yet, the Department of Literature at AU had been especially generous to me. My stint as a teaching assistant had left me with decent teaching skills. I could keep my tech job and become an adjunct; perhaps save a little and negotiate for extra time off my tech job in the summer. And so I accepted what came to me and signed on the bottom line. For a pittance, I would try teaching an introductory course in creative writing for one semester at the university.

Who knew? I loved it. I loved being in the classroom, creating ways to bring the students around to loving the process, exposing them to brilliant writing, and guiding them through the how-to of improving their own.

Why is it that you're the last one to get the picture that is forming of your own life? I had taught at AU for two semesters when another writer friend teaching at the Corcoran School of Art suggested I apply for an adjunct position there. Now I had adjunct positions at two schools and the laboratory job working over weekends.

Then yet another phone call and another tip about an adjunct position. This time it was at George Washington University, the place where I had taken my first writing workshop. With my MFA, some teaching experience, and a book in hand, I was hired to teach one workshop. After a year, I was offered an additional workshop. The giving-ness of the universe is endless, already given. During spring break that year, a tenure-track assistant professor position was posted at GWU, and I jumped through all the formal and necessary hoops it took to claim it as mine.

By the summer of my second year of full-time teaching at George Washington University I had been reasonably productive. Toward tenure I could boast sufficient publication of individual poems, essays, and articles. The university wanted from me what I wanted for myself—to continue to publish well.

Summers were best when I was off the clock and had the possibility of uninterrupted writing time. I had been enjoying my recent departure from poetry to write short stories, though the poetry fundamental to my voice still held sway. I had deep gratitude for the sacred act of being lost in creative expression. Often, as a purely spiritual exercise amazing in its fluidity, whole pages poured forth, outside of rational thinking. Language flowed like a song I did not know but found myself humming. By that summer, I had been working on six or seven stories, and a couple had been published in literary magazines.

On a July day, I sweltered in the literature tent at Artscape, the Maryland arts festival. I was there autographing my small, 22-page chapbook, *October Brown*, which I had read aloud the night before during the awards ceremony. My story had won the Artscape Award, and chapbook publication—50 copies—was the prize.

In whatever meager ways I was capable then, I had seized every opportunity to further my intention to publish another book. For my fiction collection, I had created a simple affirmation. In the clothes closet I opened every morning, I had posted my vision board with a cameo cut-out of my own profile deep in meditation. I had images of awards and prize-winning books, images of fistfuls of large-denomination bills. My mental atmosphere was to allow—as much as I could—the process to unfold. Despite blank pages and blank days, I pictured myself reading before a large crowd.

That July day at Artscape, I had brought my own webbed lawn chair to scoot up to the tiny table that approximated a booth. The arrangement allowed each of us—writers, small publishers, agents, editors—space to converse with our public, sell magazines, sign up subscribers, pitch to whomever necessary.

I had brought along a small box containing the pink flyers advertising the festival, a few literary magazines that I had purchased, my Granny Smith apple, and my water bottle. I had set the box on the ground beside my chair, and for most of the afternoon I stood, happily autographing my chapbook for anyone who paid the four dollars.

A few people had gathered, and were picking up chapbooks from the stack on my table, thumbing through the pages. I stood in front of my chair and greeted each person who approached. The group fell into a short line, money in hands.

One by one, they paid for their chapbooks, and I asked, "Would you like me to sign?" I got each name, autographed the book, and bid them goodbye with, "Enjoy!"

Somewhere mid-afternoon, a woman came up. Though I recall the gist of the conversation, I don't remember her appearance, and so for purposes here, she was ordinary-looking, with straight brown hair and a pleasant face. Let's say she wore a beige linen skirt, with the kind of cotton-blend white top that allowed the collar to fall softly without a creased lapel. She handed me the book and some bills. I took them and opened the book's front cover.

I asked, "Is this for you?"

"Yes," she said, and before I could ask her name, she told me how much she had enjoyed the story I'd read the night before. I thanked her, and readied my pen.

"How long have you been writing?" she asked.

"Fiction? Not very long," I told her. "But I've published a collection of poems."

"Oh," she said. "What's the title?"

The short line behind her was growing. People were fanning themselves and shading their eyes with their hands. I gave her the title of my collection.

"Have you published many stories?" she asked.

"Just a couple," I said. "Spell your name so I'll get it right."

"What magazines?" she asked.

I told her about the small presses where I published the stories. The others were getting impatient. I was getting impatient.

"You have many other stories?"

I could see that she wouldn't be satisfied until she got whatever the information was that had her pushing.

"Yes; as a matter of fact, I'm working on a collection."

"Do you have an agent yet?"

At this point, I ignored the question and got back to the business at hand.

"How would you like me to address your book?"

"Okay, but I know a good agent. Her name is Molly Friedrich and she's in New York. You should send her your stories."

Everyone knows someone who knows someone who chanced upon a great agent or a sorry one. I could not be bothered about getting an agent. I did not know this woman, and she was taking too much time.

I nearly dismissed her with, "Thanks. Now how would you like me to sign your book?"

"Jackie," she said. As I signed, "For Jackie," she said again, "You should send your stories to Molly in New York."

"Okay, maybe I will," I said, and handed her the autographed book, looking to the next person in line.

She insisted, "Well, write it down."

"Just like that?" My voice had an edge. "Just send my stories to someone I don't know and who doesn't know me?"

"Tell her I told you to send them."

I tore off one corner of a pink flyer and wrote "Molly Friedrich NY."

"Who shall I say suggested this?"

"Just say Jackie," she said. Finally she turned to walk away. I called after her, "You have a last name?"

"She threw back over her shoulder, "Just say Jackie."

And she was gone. I never saw her again. I tossed the pink scrap of paper into the box beside my chair and greeted my next customer.

In October, a friend and colleague badgered me about sharing the short-story manuscript I had been polishing. I shared it, she appraised it, and she sent it to her own editor at one of the top publishing houses. It was returned with a warm, encouraging letter. I thought about the woman, Jackie, who months before had given me the name of a supposed New York literary agent.

In my basement, where accumulations of quasi-important, unsorted items can remain in various unmarked boxes for years, I uncovered my summer box from Artscape. Magazines were splayed across bits of trash, a jumble of pink flyers, and a wrinkled scrap of pink paper. I seized the scrap. "Molly Friedrich NY," it read.

From directory assistance, I got a New York address. I wrote a note explaining that—although cryptic—a person who had called herself "Jackie" had suggested that I send my stories to her. As was the custom, I included a self-addressed, stamped envelope, and asked that if, indeed, she was a literary agent and was not interested, to please return the manuscript.

A few weeks went by. Then I received a small, thank-you-note-sized envelope with the return address "Molly Friedrich, Aaron Priest Literary Agency." Inside, her note informed me that uncommon as it was for her to read manuscripts that have come "across the transom," she was reading mine and would soon be in touch. Shortly thereafter, she phoned and asked when it would be convenient for me to come to New York. I was ecstatic.

The Wednesday before Thanksgiving, I made the trip to meet Molly Friedrich. She was perplexed about who the woman, Jackie, could have been. Over lunch at a lovely restaurant near Grand Central Station, I was amazed by her prodigious knowledge of books and writing. Even more awesome, she had an uncanny sense of what it means to be a writer who wants not merely to publish, but to share the whole enchilada—the language, the story, the deeper meanings. At the end of lunch, just to be certain that this was truly a godsend, I asked, "Does this mean that you're my agent?"

Big laughter spilled out of her. Later, I came across articles that described her as a force of nature in the publishing world. "Yes," she said and gave me clear instructions.

"Your job is to write. So go home and get started on your next thing." She explained that she would shop my collection around the publishing houses, and if no one was interested, she would ask me to send her something else.

"Euphoric" does not convey what I felt. Having a New York agent was the most exciting thing that had happened to me and my new career, and it had a beyond-this-world cast to it.

A few weeks later, on the last day of the fall semester, I turned in grades and checked my voicemail. Molly had left the message that she had no takers thus far, that nothing much happens over the holidays. She would be in touch early in January.

That same evening, when I arrived home, she had left another voicemail. No matter what time I arrived home, I was to phone her. I leapt for the telephone. The news: three publishing houses were interested in my book. I needed to be in New York the next morning at 9:00 a.m. to begin a round of interviews. And after the interviews, I would choose the editor and the publishing house I preferred. Major big deal.

By the time Molly got this much across to me, I was literally screaming in joy and amazement. Calmly, she instructed me to hang up the telephone and collect myself. She suggested that I get pen and paper to write down her instructions, and in 10 minutes, she would phone me again. In a frenzy, I obeyed.

The next day, my daughter and I took the train to New York. One of my sons had moved there, and they would cross their fingers while I had my whirlwind meetings with editors.

As previously arranged, every few hours I checked in with Molly, the quintessential advocate and guide through the publishing world. With her behind-the-scenes negotiating throughout the day, I made my choice. I have to say here how wondrous it was to get a hello from the universe when I was in the company of the right editor for my book. As I sat in the potential editor's office having a seemingly inconsequential conversation, she asked me why, in my manuscript, some characters had full stories and some did not. Suddenly I was overwhelmed with the perfect knowing of yet-to-be-written stories that would ultimately interconnect to form the overarching narrative that was intended.

The contract I received for my first fiction book was secondary to me. What was primary was that I had crossed the desert. Finally, I would share my way of speaking with the whole world. I felt like a writer. I felt it was not just something I did, but something I was; as if inside I had always been a writer. Now I, and everyone else, could experience the channel I was meant to create.

As it turned out, my book, *Rattlebone*, was published to good reviews in all the major newspapers. It won several prestigious awards, including the *Chicago Tribune*'s Heartland Prize. Molly Friedrich negotiated all of this, as well as international rights. In the dedication section of the book I included, "For the angel Jackie, wherever you are."

The real story here is the deliberate process required for bringing a no-thing idea into existence as something. Everything necessary for success can come without strife—an agent, an editor, a publisher, the perfect fit. And not just a book, not just a big splash of recognition and prosperity. But also the process, and the awareness of how it goes on. By whatever common name, creativity remains an amazing thing.

When you have developed the channel through which you express yourself, you get up every morning and go to bed each night grateful to have, ongoing, an absolutely essential activity. Becoming one with your expression, you are more you than you have ever been. Nothing is needed to complete you; you are more than enough; you harmonize with everything and everyone. When you are at one with this thing, and recognize your oneness with all that is, bliss can follow. You radiate and have reflected back to you the life-affirming attitudes that renew your body, mind, and spirit. And you have a map.

For anybody who has grown accustomed to the stretching, the reaching, and the touching of markers along the way, landing in this place can be heady.

On one level, success can satisfy your human need to say "I am." The world attributes supreme value to achievement and status. That worldly view of becoming more valuable may attract a good deal of attention—fame, even.

The human need for validation cannot be overstated: praise confirms your connection with others as inspirations, as mirrors, or as fellow travelers. Genuine appreciation can assure you that you put out there exactly what you intend. The shift in prosperity can be a bonus that contributes to your well-being in unexpected ways.

But there is more, something deeper. Consider the healing effects of doing what you love. The mind-body connection becomes clear as your mental faculties are sharpened. Your confidence is off the chart, and your emotional balance is steady. Now, more courageous than ever, you engage that "thing," and energy surges throughout your body, revving up your vitality. Your sense of purpose upgrades the overall quality of your life. Acceptance of the giving-ness reigns.

Passion has kept you going. Each day you awaken with can't-wait-to-do-this joy. Each step has inspired the next and the next until you have extended beyond what you may have imagined possible.

Honor this time. You lived with the hunger, the disquiet, and the dream. You had the courage to choose, and opened to a way to speak. You had the love to commit to your heart-call and the faith to follow through on your part. The point is that, whether or not you were aware of any principle, the principle worked for you because you allowed it to do what it does.

The foreign country that you once entered is now home base. You know the language, the dialects, the nuances.

This is your life. This *is* your life. This is *your* life. This is your *life*. Celebrate!

The Map

Lofty words about the transformative power of conscious creative expression may have resonated with you at some point. You may have long known what it means to be lost in the sense of timelessness when you are fully absorbed in an activity. Everywhere you look, you may clearly observe an idea that has come into form, enriching lives. Mentally, you may understand all the principles and be grateful that they exist.

Nothing, however, convinces like experience. Once you plumb the depths of your own creative impulse and transform invisible energy into something visible, you have demonstrated a self-evident truth about your essential being and the creative power of belief.

Everything that exists existed first as a thought, an idea, an intention—to infinity. Having consciously manifested a unique way of expressing creativity, you have inscribed how to leap from here to there in your brain's neural map, and in your heart's well of memory. Like a seasoned cartographer, you have scouted out the territory with all its seas and elevations. Your new, inner-self identity makes transformation a foregone conclusion. Your frequency now resonates with what you are rather than what you do. People, things, and events no longer attuned to your vibration have fallen away, and new ones arise.

What you have delivered is your deliverance. As you have come to realize more fully who and what you are, you can live from that realization. New ways of seeing make clear the inextricable connections between all aspects of your entire life, which is more than the sum of the parts.

Think of arrival at creative self-expression as a newly painted wall of a room. By comparison, the other walls show up as flawed, in need of attention. This is about a tipping point. Your experience of life tips the rest of it one way or another. The energy-of-being reaches critical mass and a fundamental shift occurs in the whole of your life.

In fact, if we acknowledge that the experience of love, peace, joy, harmony, abundance, wholeness is at the core of our deepest longing, we can see how expression in some way is always addressing that core desire. The only difference is that we now know how to do it consciously.

Whatever you want—to reach physical, mental, or spiritual well-being; to attain financial freedom; to uplift others—you will have had the experience of using what is yours to use in the universe. Lifestyle, then, serves that inner greatness against which nothing can prevail. You have become what you always were.

No wonder the monarch butterfly is such a common symbol for transformation: every step of its process of becoming is laden with metaphorical resonance. First, the female lays a single egg on a leaf of milkweed. Instinctively, she does this on a plant that is poisonous to other creatures. It makes the perfect environment for the egg's ultimate development: once the egg hatches, the tiny, voracious caterpillar eats milkweed continually. In this land of plenty, the caterpillar grows to a thousand times its hatch-weight. In the process of digesting milkweed, its body becomes poisonous to predators. The very thing that nurtures the caterpillar renders it invincible.

As the caterpillar grows, it must shed its outer skin four or five times to accommodate the changes in size and shape. From time to time, tiny structures— "imaginal" cells—crop up in its body, and are wiped out by an immune system that is waiting for the pivotal moment. It is only later that the imaginal cells come up with greater strength and encounter less resistance. They grow toward their ultimate purpose. Little by little, the caterpillar casts off whatever does not fit in the overall scheme of things.

When the time comes, it spins its own silk pad, attaches the pad to a solid branch, and hangs there for a brief time-out—like the bridge between what was and what will be.

In this still time, the awesome metamorphosis begins. The caterpillar convulses, breaks off its outer skin, sheds its 16 legs and its head capsule; it gives up the body it once occupied. This gives rise to a chrysalis, and the caterpillar enters this stage without the vision of the simple eyes it once had. Within the cocoon now, the inner parts of the caterpillar simply dissolve. The old systems that once sustained it give way to a new potential. Only the tiny heart remains intact. The resistant immune system has shut down, and the imaginal cells—wondrous preliminary cells to the body of a butterfly—now begin their rapid development into a completely different insect.

At the appointed interval, the caterpillar increases its strength by struggling to free itself from the chrysalis. It now has compound eyes that are sensitive to color. Finally, it spreads the four magnificent wings of the full-grown butterfly it has become, a new creature, flying at will.

And there is more. The monarch butterfly is unique in the way its legendary migration is mapped in its being and shared over generations. Its life cycle—egg, caterpillar, chrysalis, and adult—makes up one generation. Each year, there are four generations of butterflies. Each of the first three generations lives up to twelve weeks, then lays eggs and dies.

The fourth generation—the last one in the year—has an entirely different experience. It goes through its life cycle just as the three generations before it. When the adult butterfly emerges from the chrysalis, however, its life extends five to seven more months. This fourth generation is on a mission. Before it lays eggs and dies, this fourth generation is the adult population that makes the migration—2,500 miles—that is unique in the whole of the animal kingdom.

All generations before it have vanished, so how is it that each fourth generation knows? It appears to be led by an inscrutable inner compass to exactly the same place, by exactly the same route as successive fourth—not second or third—generations before it. Members of the fourth generation hibernate over winter. Some return to their northern home, and others lay eggs and die along the way. New second and new third generations hatch, continue the journey for a few weeks, and die, but they give rise to fourth-generation butterflies with navigational systems that bring them to their birthplace. How awesome that all the necessary knowledge has been transferred as if all generations of butterflies—living and dead—share one mind, one map, one journey, one destination. Each fully realizes its part, which contributes to the amazing feat of the entire swarm.

Cultivating Gratitude

People say that the practice of gratitude is the strongest link to well-being. Your gratitude will bring you face to face with the gifts you give and with your openness to giving more. Those who say this know that at this stage of completion thankfulness for arrival arises spontaneously within you. Amid accomplishments, you might develop the tendency to be grateful only for major events and experiences. Smaller things—the genuine smile you received from the person at the DMV counter—may slip beneath your attitude radar. Your appreciation for the smallest of gestures gets you focusing on the abundance of things that you take for granted, but that light up your existence. This is how you develop a grateful attitude toward life.

Being in continual touch with gratitude keeps you looking for the kernel of good that is always at the core of a challenge. It makes you more aware of how much you have been given. The people, the places, the help, the knowledge, the money—you could make a list each day over years and never repeat a single thing. Everything we receive—tangible and intangible—is given to us, whether it is asked for or unasked for. You cannot "earn" it. The giving-ness of the universe is without condition, even when you aren't aware that it is pouring out in your direction.

This may be the ideal juncture to begin keeping a gratitude journal. In addition, try any of these exercises:

1. Each night, make a list of at least five things—the small and large gifts you received that day—for which you are grateful.

2. Affirm the truth of your completion, celebration and gratitude. For example:

> *I am so grateful that I have (creative activity), which fulfills me, rewards me, and allows me to express and share myself.*
>
> *I am lifted and ever expanding in love that gives rise to all my thoughts, words, and activities.*

3. Create a ritual of completion and celebration. A part of it should include one or one hundred friends and family with whom you would like to share it. Include things to symbolize completion: blooming plants, ripe fruit, celebratory music, candlelight (letting light shine), etc. Make it yours. This is a good time to send out expressions of gratitude as well as invitations. In the celebration ceremony, your expression of genuine gratitude will be willingly received.

4. Cement the habit of having TEA (Time, Energy, Attention) with only your "friends." Your friends are any thoughts, beliefs, actions, words, or attitudes that support any aspect of your new creative expression.

Cultivating Forgiveness

When you've moved on to a greater expression, there is still more to be done. If you're on task, you recognize that in order to tell your story of overcoming and empowerment, there must always be the wounding and despair you are tempted to convey because it came first. To move on in ease and freedom is to release the struggle that bought you to that door; to allow the wounding to fall away.

I had yet to touch that. I don't remember launching a campaign of forgiveness for my ex-husband. I do remember years of holding clear boundaries when civility was all that I could manage between us. It seemed that anything beyond that would convey that all was forgiven. For a long time, all was not forgiven.

I wanted him to understand how inhumane he had been, and be sorry. I wanted him to hang a stone of regret around his neck to remind him. I wanted him to understand the depth of my wounds and to acknowledge the details of his crimes against me. Several times over the years when he apologized, he spoke in sweeping generalities, and his language seemed pro forma, seldom touching on what I thought I needed in order to forgive him. I came to believe that he could not fathom or appreciate what I had experienced.

Then came my vague weariness of lugging around the heaviness of anger and resentment. I remember not wanting to be identified with the woman I had once been, and wanting to bury the story. There were times that—for my own sake—I wanted to forgive him, but I didn't know how to do that. Perhaps just wanting to was enough. Ultimately, I moved my mind's focus from that old life to the life that I was building, and the past began to recede. The facts remained, but the emotional payoff—the anger and resentment that fueled my moral-high-road stance—began to dissipate. Until I could let go of my need for him to be, say, or do anything, I was bound to the dregs of that unhealthy connection.

Forgiveness is not so much about the other person as it is about releasing that thing in us that insists it must hold on to past hurts. Facts may remain, but your identification with them wants to dissolve. Those people, events, places, and experiences that were the vehicles of past hurts are the things to which we once gave power. The dredged-up feelings will wield their power for as long as we hold on to them. As long as we rehearse stories about the past, those attitudes will block the way to the peaceful, joyful, abundant, harmonious, expressive lives we want.

I remember my first awareness that some measure of forgiveness had already taken hold. I had not consciously affirmed it, nor worked at forgiving him, but for my own peace, I had wanted to be done with that. It was the Saturday before a Mother's Day. For several years, flowers had arrived from him for my birthday or for Mother's Day. Up until then, usually I ignored the gesture and threw them away. This time, the note conveyed gratitude from him to me for being the mother that I was to our children. My reaction was a surprise of tears. I couldn't make sense of it, but it was the beginning of the end of my contempt. In my eyes, he was becoming a man I once knew who had shortcomings and issues that perhaps had come with his own childhood survival story, which had had nothing to do with me. Soon his existence would no longer hold a charge, negative or positive. It was the beginning of forgiving myself, too, for living the way I did for so many years, not valuing myself.

Forgiving yourself can open a can of worms. When you consider the whole of your life, your own faults and mistakes can sweep away any substantial claim to moral high ground. Looking at the slights, betrayals, pain, and offenses that, intentionally or not, you have inflicted on others can be a part of that sobering process. Guilt and regrets can weigh heavily. But all that, too, can fall into an appropriate place with acceptance of yourself as a human being, with all the messiness and frailty that entails. And so you make amends as much as you can, apologizing when and where you can, and honoring the lessons learned.

When forgiveness is in order, whether of another or of yourself, you employ everything at your disposal—knowledge, professional expertise, heart, time, will, imagination, creativity, and, above all, spiritual practices—to get it done. The one who forgives stands to gain the lion's share of peace. Over time you may come to discover that some of the very souls whom you once thought did not "deserve" your forgiveness turned out to be unwitting facilitators in your expansion.

As you develop this heart-call in the world, you don't want to diminish the power of your expression. It can support the healing of the wound you experienced or inflicted on another, and help you realign with the energy of wholeness where forgiveness is the norm. If forgiveness is something you have yet to do, consider a few things:

- Remember that you are a valuable, worthwhile, magnificent being no matter what anyone else thinks or thought, says or said, does or did; *and* no matter what you, yourself, think or thought, say or said, do or did.
- Plenty of professional help is available.
- Forgiveness is not the same as condoning; you don't forget what happened.
- Feelings are not facts. You are not your pain and anger. Forgiveness means that you are letting the pain and emotional weight of whatever occurred fall away from you.
- The past is gone and cannot be retrieved. In order to get a fresh perspective on someone who has brought injury to you, think of who the other person was as a baby. At some point, that person was innocent and trying to learn how to be in the world, just as you were. People make mistakes, and sometimes they cannot admit that. What the person said or did was more about that person and his or her issues than it was about you. The other person may never be willing to change.

- You may need to articulate what happened and how you felt or feel about it. If so, write a letter to the offending person, using great detail and honesty. Then burn the letter, symbolically releasing all of that.
- If you are wanting to be forgiven, ask for it. Apologize for the hurt you caused, whether or not the person is still on the planet. Make reparations in any way you can without infringing on the rights or lives of other people.
- Move on.

In his popular book *Radical Forgiveness*, Colin Tipping has written an in-depth study of the process. Remember, you are clearing out flawed thinking in every aspect of your life and replacing it with the true reality. Lack—of imagination, ideas, possibilities—has no power.

More grows in the garden than the
gardener knows he has sown.
—Spanish Proverb

8
SHARING IS THE BEST PART

Just as we do not compel our own hearts to beat, we do not put the heart's desire into our own consciousness. The creative idea that is given to us is related to our soul's purpose. It's like a promise. We can be assured of full realization because the impulse toward completing it is already in us. As we become the thing we love to do, we engage the entirety of our essential self and our personality.

Ever since language became a human faculty, we humans have tried to articulate the peak experiences of pure connection, expansiveness, deep comprehension, super-human strength, genius, and the like. In our collective language, we have adopted terms that attempt to convey those sacred experiences. "God is love" is but one poignant example.

Harmony, peace beyond understanding, unlimited supply, joy beyond measure, infinite intelligence, wholeness—all are self-evident good experiences we associate with the Infinite and our connection to It. Ultimately, because we use descriptive terms for the indescribable, we have come to recognize our ground-of-being as Love, Peace, Joy, Wholeness, and such.

The heart's desire, the vessel that we bring into form, is linked to these self-evident-good qualities. When we commit to creating a channel through which the life force rushes, we commit to out-picture attributes of the sacred. Call it talent, work, genius, art, or gift—when we are at one with it, we are in the place where state-of-being and ground-of-being are one. The Infinite is being expressed by means of us in our chosen way.

Thus a musician's mastery of the flute may signify an alignment with beauty, clearing the way for greater expression of harmony. An inventor's intuitive knowing that the answer is contained in the question may out-picture infinite intelligence, an attribute of the essential self. The sense of meaning and purpose that comes with serving others in healing arts suggests compassion, while genuine commitment to home-making can reflect a love of order. Whatever the conscious creative expression, it is linked to the core of our being.

When you express your thing, you automatically share it. Sharing means giving, and giving means giving way to the flow of attributes through your unique channel. The Infinite gives Itself into and out of form eternally, which makes creation ongoing and continuous—for us and for our expression. The experience of giving is the experience of being in the flow. And so your individual giving-ness need not be finite. You need not hold back, or hold onto. You can honor and respect your gift, and with abandon, spend it. It is impossible to save it or store it up to be given piecemeal.

Once you manifest your thing, your cup is filled. Yet it is the running-over cup that bestows the essential sweetness of life. The act of being at one with your expression and allowing it to flow into this world with no resistance—that is the gift. The Infinite, as you, is channeled through a fathomless complex of body, mind, and being that involves more than any human could ever pull together. It is all supremely coordinated to deliver a blessing to the world.

And so this whole process stirs new attitudes, generates new abilities, and expands your faculties. The deeper sensibility you allow points you in the direction of higher ground where, by grace, you are lifted into greater awareness.

From there, ever-greater ideas press to come into form. Those manifestations turn out to be the "outside-the-box" activities of our lives. The world uses labels like "progress," "innovation," "invention," and "human endeavor," all of which speak to evolutionary genius. And so as we claim, develop, and share who and what we are, the raising of the frequency of the entire collective is already handled.

You can see how sacred service is wrapped up in sharing. By definition, sacred service is all about service you give with no expectation of praise or tangible reward. This kind of service is held in reverence because it is associated with harmony, kindness, compassion, peace, abundance, etc. Many of us talk about our creative expression as a calling, a heart-call. By spiritual agreement, we feel drawn to a particular arena or activity. Sharing can be your sacred service. Once again, to express freely is to share, and to share is to give. There are as many ways to share selflessly as there are people. I was the daughter of one.

There is an old saying in African-American culture, "Every shut eye ain't sleepin', every goodbye ain't gone." Until my mother left the planet, I had never thought much about what that saying meant. And I was probably not unique in my ignorance about the grieving process. I believed that seeing my mother through her lengthy illness and then feeling a mix of relief and sadness at her death meant that my grief was over. Everything was done; I needed to move on. Not so. There was still work to do with the mind-frame that held my story of our relationship, and the universal significance of her sharing her gift.

Usually I took pleasure in the view out my bedroom window: the graceful slope of a hill, the trees and small patch of sky that greeted me each dawn. That September morning, as I sat quietly in the chair near the window, I attributed the somber view to my change of mood. The leaves had not yet fully changed colors, but their green vibrancy had gone dull. The pungent smell of decay seeped through the crack of my raised window, and hastened that last brilliant flourish before leaves crumble into mulch.

It was a Wednesday—a non-teaching day for me—and my habit was to wrap a throw around my shoulders and contemplate morning rituals: a page from *Daily Word*, scribbles in my journal, prodding myself toward peace of mind. Though I still experienced a certain heaviness, I did not believe it to be grief. Six months had passed since my mother's death. If I was to get on with my life, I would have to be more dedicated in my spiritual practices.

I folded my legs and tried to focus on my breath. In the restless jumble of thoughts before whatever awareness might come, I had the sudden recollection of a recent magazine article about two young girls who had written a letter to their father after he had committed suicide.

Startled by the blast of a new idea, I leapt up from my chair, flung aside my blanket, and dashed down the hallway to my study. Delicate, onion-skin stationery seemed inadequate; a yellow legal pad and black ink seemed right.

With a singular focus, I was back in my chair, thoughts brimming and spilling out so quickly that my pen could hardly catch them on the page.

Dear Mom, I wrote, *I am writing to you because I haven't been able to find the peace I want whenever I think about your life and death. My feelings seem to get stuck in not accepting your life as it was. I wish always that you could have lived differently... and not felt so alone and ashamed and resentful.*

A familiar anguish ballooned in my chest; the old image loomed of her at the piano, playing and singing "Lord Jesus," tears streaming. I saw the mother I loved crying out to be saved, and thought of how it had fallen to me to be her savior. With all the attendant emotions, the past immediately became the present.

After the first few sentences on the yellow page, I was weeping. That image—my mother pregnant, singing her sorrowful gospel as she waits for my father to return with an appropriate dress for her to wear to the funeral of his father—ultimately had become a trope for all that was wrong in our family. To me it had once represented all that was perplexing about life in general, and all that was assailable in the religion my family claimed.

In my letter, I didn't have to spell out the fact that I had rejected aspects of religion. My mother had always known that my quarrel with religion had sent me on a crusade. She had seen it as a warp in my vision.

I tried many times in so many ways to tell you how to change things. I tried to share whatever would make you happy or proud. I don't think you could ever really hear. You seemed locked away in your own private prison...unwilling to be free. You didn't believe you could have a different life. You were afraid to try.

In such a paradox of blood and independence, cell memory cannot easily be cast off. Certainly I claimed the legacy of my mother's gospel and jazz music. Those cadences had pumped through my veins, and came to bless the poetry of my own voice on the written page. But also, they echoed a sense of powerlessness, a victim sensibility that I had come to resent like the dirge one rails against.

As I wrote my letter, I was so thoroughly immersed in the need to get it all out that I never digressed into gratitude. Somewhere just short of conscious thought, I allowed what I knew to be true: that "first music" opened in me an affinity for all manner of music and language. Perhaps if I had paused long enough, I would have come up with more of what was good, the happier times when she delighted in a particular accomplishment by one of her children.

But that morning, caught in the drama of autumn and loss, and writing for some kind of deliverance, I could not dwell on accomplishments. After all, she had always known that I loved her music. With gratitude, I had given her the glory with each book I wrote. Though time might heal, it can also turn sorrow to bitterness.

I always hoped you would be happy...and somewhere in me I feel thwarted. Nothing I tried really ever worked.... Right now I'm trying to find a way to let go of these old and useless frustrations about responsibility for solving your life.

I was remembering numerous times in the dance that was our bond when I arranged what I considered to be a support: the right counselor, the articles I sent, books, tapes. And I was remembering the airline ticket to the seminar, and the long hours spent on the telephone listening to the litany of ways she bore the burdens of her life. My inventory of excruciating details didn't hold sway. Frustration and failure were my companions.

I think you decided not to live years ago, and finally death said...you seemed relieved to know that you were leaving this life, and for me it meant that there would be no more chances to change your life, that the door was closing, that you waited for a magical thing to transform your life and it didn't happen. I saw you reach out to death as the only way out.

I was caught in the unyielding moments of the June day when I first got the news, "inoperable." We had gone home to Kansas, all nine of us with a sprinkling of in-laws. When we encircled the bed in the room that was hers alone for much of her married life, my father had stood in the doorway, as if crossing the threshold was a sin.

We had sung the songs that were second nature to us, "Lord, I will lift mine eyes to the hills, knowing my help is coming from you..."

Propped on pillows, my mother had fairly glowed. When the song was over, and tearfully, one by one, we had thanked her for all that she had given us, she broke it up with, "Don't you all cry."

Her tone and her expression had suggested that she was perplexed by our grief. She had even smiled when she said, "I'm free now." Casually, she had looked around and said, "It's over."

There had been the discussion about her care and what she wanted or needed.

"One thing," she had told us. "I don't want to be in the hospital, and I don't want to ever be alone."

We had devised a schedule to ensure that by plane or train or car, one of us would always be in the house to help with her care. Initially, in the days that followed, she had been euphoric.

And so, Mom, you died. You seemed determined to do it on your own terms, never looking back, being released from a bad situation, never seeing that it might have been different. I think you did come to understand that we loved you, that we were always in this together and that we wouldn't let you leave here, standing alone on this shore. Your last three days, I was there. I sat with you, held your hand, touched you and attended to everything I could think of. I felt then and now that I saw you to the very edge of this life, and watched you push off into the next. You were never that interested in me helping you live more fully, but you really needed me to help you get through dying, and I did. I hear you saying Thanks, Mac. And I'm saying You're welcome, Mom.

Right at this point, in my bedroom in Washington, DC, something extraordinary happened. I sensed no special stillness, heard no ethereal voices and saw no flashes of light. However, the concrete reality of writing a letter changed. It simply shifted. I was holding the pen, but instead of pouring out my heart in this address to my mother, clearly I was beginning to take dictation. I wrote:

You're saying—I'm all right. I'm free now. I didn't want to stay there. What I had to do was finished. Write this so that you will know it's me telling you. I don't feel any regret or anything. That's all behind me now.... I did what I was supposed to do and I'm fine. I made it.

Go on with your life. I'll come to touch you from time to time. We had this bond always and it can't ever be broken. I love you. I thank you for wanting the best for me, but God's timing was bigger than you could see. He had a purpose for me, too, and no matter what I had to go through, I fulfilled that purpose....I did mine. You do yours. I'll be here. Love you.

In that transcendent moment, I recognized the immanent shape-shifter of mind-frames. It had come as my mother's return to release me from my own misperception that I had ever been responsible for her happiness.

For so many years, with all her complaints, and all my attempts to "help" her or "fix" things in her life, small wonder that I never saw any difference. Even if the net sum of her experience had not added up to the exalted number she may have wanted, her life had been full. She had actually been saying, "Thanks, but no thanks." All that time I had seen only what I believed, and not seen the reality she must have always known.

As I sat with my yellow pad, I remembered facts that I had never allowed to contradict my story of her life. Out of her heart's desire she had managed to take a few piano lessons and taught herself to play a classical piece she adored: Debussy's "Clair de Lune." She had once used her "church" money for a lease-to-buy baby grand piano. Later in her life she had gotten her GED, which had led to a part-time job at Hallmark, which had led to trading in her piano for an organ. I remembered the photo image of her that graced the front of a Hallmark Christmas card for grandmothers.

I thought of her sharing her gift with the world, what it had brought to countless others for decades in some church every Sunday. People had been moved by her music. Countless children had wanted lessons, countless others in choirs had become musicians in their own right.

But more, I thought of the peace, the release, and the healing, in whatever degree, that must have come to her as a result of expression, of sharing her gift with others and with herself. By her very existence, she had been bound to speak, to fashion a wonderfully moving sound from no-thing save a singular impulse to pull the music of her heart, broken or not, out of thin air and make it hers.

She had never allowed anything inside or outside of herself—not her anger, not religion, not marriage or poverty, not my blind protestations or my resentment—to take away her gift. She had found a way to express her creativity, and what she delivered to the world had been her deliverance.

She had returned to leave me with a glimpse of the larger truth about her life. With it, I was also receiving a deeper comprehension of the subtlety of grace, how it can occur in retrospect, blessing lives even in the face of sorrow and discord. What is mystical territory, if not the infinite ways that the truth can be revealed to an oblivious heart?

And so, as involuntarily as we breathe, we share the gifts. For people like my mother, the attachment to an outcome is not important. Sharing transforms the giver. The sheer joy of sharing is received by any open other who happens along. Generally speaking, that part is the least of our concerns as the human question of where to express takes hold. The computer chip you dream up is divine intervention for millions. The landscape you paint speaks to some tourist's heart; your voice as the announcer soothes a baby in a car like a lullaby; your music leaves an unknown listener awestruck. The meal you prepare is an offering of love to your children. Your invention becomes a balm for humanity, on and on.

For some, the expression is incomplete without a conspicuous receiver or beneficiary. This can be dicey. If the idea of obligation is the filter through which you see sharing, the expression is not given freely. When you give without attachment, it comes from true abundance, which is not a state of having. Rather, it is a state of being, a flow state where to give is to have.

If you hold back, censoring yourself, you could be coming from the consciousness of lack. If you are waiting for what you might receive, you make your gift a commodity where the focus on "how to get" rules. If you view your wondrous expression through the limiting lens of "work" or "job," and impose a sense of striving at something you "have to" do, you are effort-ing your way into a shadow of fulfillment.

Whether or not you consciously connect with a beneficiary, the circle is always complete. For every creative expression, there is something or someone in the perfect position to receive it, to be lifted in it, transformed by it. The Infinite that has the capacity to essentially coordinate all aspects of all creation, including details of the perfect creative expression for each individual over all time, certainly has the capacity to bring together giver and receiver. Once again, laws of attraction hold sway.

Cultivating a Consciousness of Giving

Giving away something every day with no attachment to the outcome can open the heart and change our frequency. With constancy, this practice moves you into an experiential alignment with Love. You see the difference even in the ordinary skirmishes of everyday life. You end up letting people be as they are. In traffic, you let people off the hook for cutting in front of you or taking your parking space, not because you rationalize their possible motivations, but because, in that moment, you give up resistance, give your earnest acceptance of what is, and take it no further. You let it be. Peace is the dividend.

One day I found myself online browsing the archive of Ode magazine, to which I wanted to re-subscribe, and stumbled across an article entitled "It's Good to Give." The article said that giving doesn't only make you feel good, but can impact your health as well. And it went on to tell the story of Cami Walker.

In her early thirties, newly married, and working a high-powered job with an advertising agency, Cami was stricken with multiple sclerosis. She lost the use of her hands, then vision in one eye. The fatigue and numbness were debilitating. Within two years, she had quit her job, developed an addiction to prescription drugs, and become completely dependent on her husband.

One night, in a state of depression, she phoned her friend Mbali Creazzo, a South African medicine woman who drew from the Dagara African tradition and had also been a pioneer in integrative medicine in San Francisco. Creazzo prescribed a ritual: Give away 29 gifts in 29 days. Cami Walker was resistant: "I couldn't get out of bed, so how was I going to give something to someone every day?" And Creazzo told her, "It doesn't have to be material. It can be that you say something nice." Creazzo told her, "It will shift your energy for life."

On Day One, Walker decided to give the gift of her time and attention to a friend who was in a more advanced stage of MS. Her friend was ecstatic to hear from her, and they made a plan to get together. "When I hung up the phone, I felt lighter and I was smiling," she says. "And I thought, Okay, it does feel good to give. And then out of the blue, I got this phone call to do a consulting project. I took myself out to breakfast to celebrate and there was a guy who just anonymously paid for my breakfast!"

Walker continued the ritual and chronicled her amazing experiences in the 2009 *New York Times* bestseller *29 Gifts: How a Month of Giving Can Change Your Life*. On her 29th day, she launched an online challenge site to inspire a worldwide revival of the giving spirit. Some 17,000 people in 43 countries signed up.

When you become conscious that giving-ness is pouring out all over you, it feels like grace. Even before I acted, the mere idea of giving away nothing in particular every day—a word, a smile, money, things—to no one in particular was such a powerful impulse. It fit right in with my belief about the nature of true giving, just letting flow what will. I saw this as a worthy discipline, a way to live more consciously from that belief. I felt major freedom and gratitude just imagining what it would be like to hold on to nothing.

The day I sat reading was, for me, day one. Though it was not mentioned in the article, it came as a download from the universe that it would be important for me to give without attachment to any outcome. And the more anonymously I gave, the better. For years I had given time and energy to reading and editing manuscripts of former students and colleagues. Voluntarily, I had written articles for small newsletters. I had written poems and given them away for the sheer pleasure of writing. I had given time, energy and money to many groups and affiliations voluntarily, given much to those I love. Now this article was talking about impersonal, unconditional, daily giving that was or was not related to a talent.

And so I adopted the discipline. On day one, I picked up an empty potato-chip bag alongside the aisle of the grocery store. It wasn't in my path, and quickly I had to let go of the censor and the judge in me about trash, and who cleans it up. It felt uplifting just to let my initial impulse have its way for the sake of giving. On day two, I left tulips on the stoop of an acquaintance who lived 20 miles away but was housebound without a car. And on the morning of day three, I awoke to the realization that I could give away time and energy in a way I had never considered doing. I could give my time, energy, attention, and whatever else was involved. Wherever I got a yes, I could facilitate meditation.

And so on day three, I contacted a minister. On day four she said yes to allowing me to facilitate an evening meditation at her Center for whomever would come, not for the purpose of growing a congregation anywhere, or not even for the purpose of changing anybody. Not for anyone or anything outside of my own desire to be in the flow of giving without attachment. The mere idea of opening to the possibility each week of group-sitting in stillness and allowing it to be, filled me with a sense of freedom and humility, gratitude and abundance.

Day one, picking up the bag, I had had a clear shift upward. I was more accepting of myself. On the day I left the tulips, I would describe the shift as "staying with myself." The giving had nothing to do with the receiver. That same day, a publisher sent me an email to say that he was interested in the manuscript I had worked on and decided to put away, thinking it wouldn't sell. On day four the minister said yes.

On day 18, I gave someone whom I love dearly my complete honesty with no attachment to how he might respond. That very day he checked himself into a treatment and recovery facility.

If we want never to experience lacking anything at all, we have to focus on the out-picture of right thinking. In that picture we are giving away something all the time with no attachment. If we want nothing but loving relationships, we act as if, and focus on giving away a kindness, a compassion, an acceptance. Abundance? Give away your creative gift every day.

Giving-ness Exercises

Chances are, you frequently give and share both tangible and intangible things. It is common to do this when you recognize a need or when you have a request, and sometimes as an exchange for what you hope to gain. If you want to really develop the giving-ness muscle, try any or all or the following:

1. Toss away money to the wind without an attachment to who might or might not find it.

2. Give some allotted time to sharing your creative expression. Shape time and gift into a unit that you can give away with no expectation of reward or remuneration. For example, volunteer with Big Brothers, Big Sisters or a similar group. Give to high school students who want to be the entrepreneur that you are. Bring your delicious gourmet snacks to a shelter once a week. Once a year, give a free concert at your apartment complex. Or simply allow the opportunity to come to you, and then give.

3. Give something—any life-affirming thing—away each day.

4. Keep track of your giving-ness in your journal. Also journal the serendipities and synchronicities that will surely arise.

5. Affirm the joy of sharing your self with the world. For example:

Gratefully, I am carried along in the flow of giving-ness and aligned with it.

I freely live and share my expression with the world.

I am on purpose.

All limitations to my sharing are dissolved.

Pay attention.
Be astonished.
Tell about it.
—Mary Oliver

9

OPENING TO YOUR NEXT
BEST-YET-TO-BE

Now what? The question can weigh heavily if you think that you, by yourself, made it all happen. Once I was launched in a career that I loved—writing, publishing, teaching—I was clear enough to know that there was something vital I had missed in the unfolding of my success. When I now consider the chronology of my spiritual growth up until that point, I see I had embodied some sacred practices and was aware of some principles. For example, I knew that my thoughts and beliefs had been creating my life. Fine. I was aware that that was true because of the laws of manifestation, which say, essentially, that what you believe manifests in your experience. I understood, too, that those laws have relevance to how the universe works. That had all been settled to my satisfaction. I had also experienced pure awareness, the stillness underlying everything. Great. Yet, in my preoccupation with trying to be sure that I created what I wanted, I had still been scratching after something fundamental that put it all together for me.

With all the positive experiences, in my conscious mind I had still been asking, *Yes, but how did I do that?* How did this "I" become a writer, write these books, change the course of my life? How, really, do we make it happen? This was a clear indication that unconsciously I had been holding on to the belief that life happens by me or, perhaps more to the point, life happens through me. I—meaning my personality—must think it, hold it in mind, or else it cannot happen. I was the key, wasn't I, and if so, how could I possibly continue to do this?

If the personality self—loosely called the ego—believes that it alone creates, and insists on controlling the great power behind creation, either it will languish in the emptiness of "success" without fulfillment, or be unable to sustain the status quo that brings expression.

After all that time, I had still been asking, *What's God got to do with all this?* I had still been imagining some version of something more powerful than anything or anyone out there somewhere, separate from me, sending energy for me to shape into what I wanted. And I had to be very clear about what I wanted, and possibly the how-to of it. It was as if I couldn't grasp the idea of "God" for the invisible, no-thing-ness of God. I was a lone tree, trying to grasp the idea of a forest; a blade of grass grappling with the concept of a meadow.

One day I sat in my meditation chair looking out my window, and just as a blurred image clicks into perfect clarity, I knew. It came not as a thought, but as a statement of the obvious: *I am eternal.* Of course. My sense of an eternality at my core was what people were calling God. Everything is *That*.

It is present as everything everywhere all the time coming into and going out of form; both an Infinite and a Presence. There is no entity out there. There is only the indescribable Is-ness out of which everything arises and to which everything returns. I am *That*. I cannot not be worthwhile. And that's true for everyone. We are expressions of *That*, no matter what we think, say or do.

You could call it the direct knowing that comes with everyday mysticism, or you could call it one of those "duh" moments when, in retrospect, you recognize your own blindness. I felt like I had been the last one to know consciously what my whole life's experience had been pointing to all along: that there was no boundary between me and that infinite ground-of-being energy that can never be created nor destroyed. There was no separation. *That* was my essential self, I was sprung from *That*. Finally I understood more deeply the biblical *I and the Father are one*, and so many other experiences I had had over years, things that had resonated intellectually but had never sunk in.

I wanted to connect all available knowledge that could give me at least a working sense of what it means to be on a never-ending evolutionary, spiritual journey. Humbled by my ignorance, my small and limited self began to surrender to the greater truth that all along, this had been, was, and would be my sacred journey. I was living out the practicum that proved as much of a theoretical that I was capable of accepting, catching on to what I had always been, and had always been doing.

I couldn't know, nor did I need to know, the mystery of the Infinite. Later I would develop language for what I was coming to know, but just holding to the idea that "eternal" was completely unrelated to time or sequence carried me. Later, terms like "single unity" and "indescribable Infinite" would supplant the sense I had of what was beyond description yet immanently present. For that period, though, I truly could no longer relate to the limited sense of pronouns like "He" and nouns like "God." At that point in the unfolding of my understanding, because my own limited associations needed to fall away from my thinking, I needed reinforcement of this old-but-new-to-me truth.

I was ripe for a new season; the impulse to go deeper and further was at hand. Activity-wise, I didn't know what knowledge and practice might look like. Though I knew that more times than I could count the reality must have been right before me, up until that point, no person or book had ever conveyed it me. Awareness can never be bestowed.

And then there was the issue with my writing. I still loved language and ideas, but my execution in joining the two was feeling stale. In fiction I had always felt drawn to writing conflict-resolution plots, the character-driven stories where the force of who the character is is what drives the story: the character overcomes a limitation, and resolves a situation, the way life seems to happen.

I had always been clear about the importance of presenting one of life's unfortunate or dangerous situations with all the attendant human frailties. Usually you tie the character's limitation to character flaws, human things to which most people can relate. You draw the emotional aspect from your own psyche, then you dramatize the moments of truth that lead to resolution.

One feature of the type of conflict-resolution fiction that has a hypnotic hold on entertainment culture, is that tribulations are enfolded in "happy endings." Resolution assumes a finite end, and it also assumes a previous conflict. What we perceive as happy endings unfold because of what we perceive as troubled journeys. The troubled journey—brief and finite—is what captures the imagination of the reader, pushing the human desire for resolution. We're glad to see the character solve the difficulty.

As time went on, though I loved the idea that people change and resolve their issues, I couldn't seem to find a way to convey the importance of the deeper transformation—the true epiphany that is clearly metaphysical. In my fiction, the sacred couldn't be dealt with directly or the whole thing seemed to dissolve into cliché or sentimentality. Writing was still my way to express, but my desire for going more deeply into the sacred was there, and I had not a clue about how to convey it. I embarked on a novel where one of the characters had tragically made her transition before the novel unfolded, and was present on the page only as a disembodied voice. It was my clumsy effort to break my usual storytelling pattern. It sufficed to a point, but did not touch the metaphysical as deeply as I had desired.

One rainy night, I attended a lecture being held at a high school auditorium in the suburbs. As I sat waiting for the speaker to arrive—he was slated to talk about connections between the brain, the mind, and the sacred—I glimpsed a woman sitting about 10 seats away on the row in front of me. She had the face of someone I had known back in high school in Kansas, some 40 years before. I said to myself, that woman looks like she could have once been Janette Dearborn.

I set about trying to discover if, indeed, this was she. I asked that the question "Is your name Janette?" be passed down the row of strangers between us until it got to the woman in the blue sweater. I watched as each person turned and whispered and pointed. When someone tapped her on the shoulder and spoke to her, the woman in blue flashed her white teeth in a big smile, and nodded yes, which in turn reverberated as person by person turned to discover the source of the question.

I waved hello. Her puzzled expression said she didn't recognize me. The noise in the auditorium was settling down and I knew the program was about to get underway. But Janette bounced up out of her seat and scooted across the row toward me. I stood up. When she got close enough to hear, I said my maiden name, and added, "Sumner High School." We both whooped in amazement that after 40 years we should bump into each other at a metaphysical lecture in the suburbs of Washington, DC. Quickly we agreed to talk at the break.

As soon as we found each other in the lobby, she asked, "What are you doing here?," the very question on my own lips. As naturally as a song can come to mind, I told her that I was looking for something, but didn't know what; that I had felt drawn to the kind of information being presented in the lecture. And when I paused to pose the same question to her, she shared that she was presently immersed in metaphysical studies in ministerial school.

Once again, the Infinite slips right past whatever rational thinking and figuring-out habits we have. It flashes a sign— say a face from a 40-year past that says home—and reveals things to us like a divine smuggler. I understood that the question I had not yet formed was being answered in the few words she spoke. I understood that whatever I was seeking would be found in the guidepost that, intentionally or not, she was giving to me.

That very night I went online until the small hours, reading about metaphysical-studies programs and principles founded on the assumption of eternality. I found a match for my own evolving beliefs, and set about finding a way to court more knowledge. Within a month, I had begun studies that a few years later led to my spiritual life coaching practice and to writing about my metaphysical journey.

And so once again, in the second half of my life, knowing that sooner rather than later, re-direction—my term for retirement—would be staring me in the face, I was newly alive with probing, practicing, being amazed, and wanting to share it.

As we continue on the planet in the second half or third chapter of life, some part of us is gone forever. New parts are being born. More and more, we are charged with adapting to changes in the world, the culture, our bodies, and what we are capable of doing physically and mentally. Repeatedly, we find ourselves standing on the bridge between endings and whatever comes next: between retirement and a new passion, between the couples' journey and the singles' journey, between loss and newfound treasure, between doing and being.

So what do you do with the wisdom you have acquired over all those years? All that experience you've expressed, does it merely vanish into the warp we have made of time? What signs are there that indicate that the need for expression is yet upon us?

Many of us carry the belief that everyone gets to have only one "career," and when the joy of living no longer seems to flow through that expression, leisure is all that remains. Reconsider the joy and grief of endings. Reconsider the metaphor of a circle in a spiral: just as the circle appears to be coming to a close, you realize that you're looking at a turn that is actually the beginning of another open circle. So it is with conscious creative expression.

If you've come—maybe suddenly—to the end of a beautifully rewarding career and a precipice beckons, "Where to from here?," one thing is certain. In this life you can choose again and again. Your life purpose dawns continually, ever rising in complete engagement with the vast domain of creativity.

Sometimes continuing your passion in a deepening way is the answer, and you go on with it happily until you leave the planet. Others become aware of their urge to learn a new skill, their longing for a new passion, the insistent need to "give back," or simply a general discontent with daily-ness. In the second half of life, these all signify the beginning of a new circle in the spiral of creative expression.

In my high school, we had the same homeroom teacher from 9th to 12th grade, which meant she got to know us pretty well. In my graduation yearbook, my homeroom teacher wrote: "May God grant you the serenity to accept the things you cannot change, the courage to change the things you can, and the wisdom to always know the difference." Over the years I discovered that she had quoted the Serenity Prayer made popular in Alcoholics Anonymous circles. Now I claim it as the best advice I have encountered about coming to terms with what we call "aging."

In the second half of life, you hope you have cultivated the serenity of acceptance. But maybe not. On a small yet significant scale, you may find that everyday situations bring on stress—the worry and doubt that can arise from surprising quarters. I can think of nothing that can disturb the peace and dangle frayed edges like unresolved relationship issues. What can be more challenging to your plateau than a visit home to family, where relationships forged in the past have not always evolved to accommodate who you hope that you are now?

This is a place where the lesson of practicing acceptance may not be so lofty. All the fissures, the hurtful family secrets, the betrayals and resentments, can easily surface in looks and innuendo. You hope you know that all the messiness, too, is an acceptable part of who you are, and not your essence. But somehow that doesn't always suffice. Before you know it, as confident as you are in the larger world, you can be challenged to either suffer or change the framework and accept the messiness of family for what it is.

I am remembering a common but significant example. June is the month of my father's birth in Rosedale, Kansas. In the June of his 89th year, I could not ignore the important fact of his birthday. I had turned in my grades, suspended meetings, and cleared my desk—school was out.

I should have been eager to settle into my summer writing routine, but I was already bored with the novel I had started, buying into the illusion of writer's block. The metaphysical class I was anticipating wouldn't begin until fall. I should have been going to yoga twice a week and finding teasers to fortify my brain against early Alzheimer's. The motor that drove the treadmill I had been on for nine months, however, simply wouldn't crank.

Lately my father had not mentioned the chiropractor, or walking on the indoor track at the mall, but on the telephone he sounded upbeat, busy with church. My hope was that he was still his vital self. I could not know, really, until I looked into his face. Still, the last thing I wanted to do was to get on a plane to Kansas.

Six weeks before, one of my sons had phoned with plans to go to Kansas for his grandpa's birthday. "Why don't you come?" he said.

It had seemed like a good idea, and the word had spread. Within days, a couple of my sisters had reserved hotel rooms, singled out the best airline deals, and informed all related households about the best possible restaurants at which to hold a celebration for Dad. For the first time in too long since Mom's death, all of us might be together again.

The problem wasn't just the difficulty of shifting gears at the end of an academic year. For me, going to my hometown was like going into a past life, and trying to dwell in what used to be. Who wants to deal with the old rifts and battle lines within the family? Downtime and Dad-time were all that I could possibly tolerate. I simply could not get excited about trying to see past the obvious differences that divided us. I had explained and heard all the explanations I'd ever need to hear about failures and flawed life choices. I was loath to spend four days struggling to make a connection. And I was riddled with guilt for feeling this way.

I could hear my own words about how beliefs we hold for years become attitudes. I certainly had an attitude. I could hear my own explanations of how attitudes become filters for how we take on life. Words. They didn't move me one nanometer toward letting it be.

We had done pretty well for siblings born over a 22-year span, with mates, children, and grandchildren all over the country. Entire generations lie between us. We had the same issues that all humanity has, and invariably they crept into our conversations.

Many times over the years, I had gone to Kansas knowing these things, treading carefully and honoring people's sore spots and resentments. Seeing family at home was supposed to be the ultimate opening of arms, but that day I could not remember the last time their arms had seemed all that open. The wall of my resistance was almost insurmountable.

Even though I thought I had to make the trip, I put off making final plans. Weeks flew by until it was the Monday before Dad's Saturday birthday. I was supposed to leave for Kansas on Friday, and I was frustrated that I couldn't, or wouldn't, get over myself and think about the love that surely was there, or else why were we born together? I couldn't see past my doubt and fear. I told myself that families were the one practiced connection on earth, an extended exercise under favorable and sometimes not-so-favorable conditions. We raised each other, fought, cried together before we exposed ourselves to the world. Family was the place where shame and guilt first sprouted roots, but it was also where ideas about joy and responsibility had their beginnings.

I owed them, big time. I should have been thanking them for staying alive long enough for me to know this. Who did I think I was; what was my problem? People differed, so what? I was all up in the ice cream but I couldn't get the flavor.

This life is set up for each person to find her own sanctuary and the way to it, his own expression and recognition of it. No matter what you think you know, this life is set up for each of us to clear out our own jungle of attitudes and perceptions, no matter how common, no matter on how many levels. When spiritual practices and self-flagellation didn't seem to work, one way that I had learned to adjust my attitude was to go off, alone, to the ocean three hours away. Perhaps surrender is more likely there because of the sheer presence of this unambiguous force of nature, or perhaps it is because the sunrise represents an order far beyond my influence. And so I packed the car and drove to the shore.

I am probably no different than nearly every other person who has been there; witnessing a sunrise at the shore means witnessing the pageant of light along a mute horizon, where sky and water are separated by an aura of mist. At some point, your perspective can shift from being observer to being a part of the drama. I like to be up at first light, contemplating the sun as the stationary daystar that it is, still out of view, but casting the glow of its fire. I like to stand in the sand, knowing that I'm attached only by gravity's pull, and that though I am ostensibly still, I am turning headlong with a planet that is tilting. And—best moment of all—I like to see that first blinding rim of white light the precise moment that the earth is actually turning over into day. At these times I know that I am on a planet in a universe that is one of countless universes, and I can sense the relative insignificance of issues.

No sunrise rewarded me that day. It rained, sprinkled, or misted for the entire three days that I was there. Yet from the moment I first maneuvered my low-to-the-ground beach chair into the sand, and draped myself in an oversized poncho, I surrendered to whatever might come. I sat for hours, not making myself meditate, not having any particular lofty goal, thinking of little, reading an irrelevant page every now and then, intending only to sit there.

It wasn't until I left the beach that first evening that I realized I was in an altered state. Everything around me seemed more alive. I felt connected to the ocean, and, as if by a sacred osmosis, it had been nourishing me.

For the three days, I was blissfully absorbed in the experience of being at one with an immense living thing, a presence unto itself. I opened to it, felt like a part of it, and it spoke to my entire being. I had the physical sensation of a silent hum moving through me, connecting me to every molecule and drop, every wave. With gratitude, I thought that whatever came in my visit to Kansas, I would have the experience of those three days to sustain me.

On my drive back to DC, I experienced the same heightened state of awareness. Trees were like giant entities, throbbing with life at the side of the road, and I wanted to stop and sit among them. I sensed countless blades of grass, each unique and in sync with the other. Every flower was an energy and they dwelled together in a seamless whole. Later, in my journal I wrote, ...*the earth seemed suddenly teeming with life that I was with, meaning connected to, like people, actual, and more than a thought or metaphor.*

A day later, a plane ride with two sisters, and I was softer about the trip. I believed that I was ready to "endure" or "tolerate" anything. We got our rental cars and headed for the small-town, two-story Hilton Garden Inn to register and drop off our bags.

There is a poem by Rumi, called "The Guest House," in which he writes, "This being human is a guest house. / Every morning a new arrival. / A joy, a depression, a meanness, / some momentary awareness comes / as an unexpected visitor. / ....The dark thought, the shame, the malice. / Meet them at the door laughing and invite them in." He talks about accepting them all because each has been sent as a guide from beyond. When we accept the feelings we bring the light of awareness to them, which keeps us in the present moment, our moment of power. I didn't believe that I had consciously accepted my cynicism, but I was willing to stop courting and fighting it. And then came the giving-ness we can never deserve or manipulate. I call it grace.

At the desk in the lobby we spotted our sister from Minnesota; we each saw each other at the same precise moment. I don't know what it is that makes people scream at moments like these, but we were lighting up the whole first floor. She looked fabulous with her new haircut and wearable-art skirt. She was so alive. We were suddenly a single body in motion, up to our rooms, tossing in suitcases, putting on walking shoes, and down the elevator again, taking one car to Dad's house.

My son answered Dad's front door, and right behind him—our father. I felt he was like an unwitting captain of our ship who, by example, had taught us how to navigate the necessary breakers and honor the wind. He was the same solid man as he had been the year before, only more intensely so. I saw his face, and in one fell swoop I knew that it was

exactly right that I was there, that my coming was the ac-
knowledgement to myself of our connection, what he was to
me. I was perplexed about the resistance I had felt.

Although I had shared my reservations about going home
with no one, I sensed that we all might have had reservations, and we all might have been shoving them aside for
this. Perhaps each of us, in our own time, had come to know
the ways that life rewards us, ways that I had taken so much
for granted, and ways that I had not been able to articulate.

We crowded around him, hugging, picking apart his out-
fit: a great shirt, beige; with slacks, matching beige socks, and
Weejuns. He liked us. Later he would show off the "sharp"
leather belt he got for next to nothing at the Swap and Shop. I
was simply grateful for the moment of grace. My son beamed
as he stood aside watching his grandfather embrace us, and
we pulled him in.

In the living room, I saw that Dad had shampooed the
carpet and bought new scatter rugs. Out back, time had begun to weather the wooden ramp he had built with his own
hands so that my mother's wheelchair could get to the curb.

Then it was Friday night and we had driven in a caravan of
six cars to a buffet to participate in the Welcoming Event. We
were in the big parking lot of a strip mall, and before my sister
could park our car, I saw my brother walking up to us, my
whole life written all over him, laughing at the bald miracle of
us seeing each other again. I was out of the car grabbing him.
That stunning glimpse of blood kin. Primordial. Amazing.
And then here came the aunts, two of my mother's remaining
sisters, wearing my mother's hair, calling my name in the lilt
of her voice, claiming me as theirs. What can you do but hug
and weep? Then more cars and more brothers and sisters, in-
laws and cousins, nieces, nephews, hands coursing over faces,
tears steaming in laughter and deep recognition.

Inside a party room at the restaurant, 40-plus of us tried talk, eat, and touch each new person who came through the door. When it was late, when we'd had our momentous first look, our first repast, and our relatives had gone home for the night, we went to our hotel, anticipating the birthday bash at the house the next day.

I spent much of the night in reflection about my initial resistance; how I had left my beach retreat hoping that the memory of a blissful time would get me through the weekend. And how instead, unknowingly, I already had the very thing that was required—acceptance. Love was always there. Changing my mind had come through grace, the giving-ness that had coordinated all the rest. I needed only to allow myself to be present in the moment, accept the moment for what it was. The whole of my visit home was an exercise in acceptance, and the reward of really connecting with the people I love.

I had forgotten that beyond the limitations of my mind, oneness was possible not only at the ocean or in solitude, but also, despite conflict and distraction, in the busyness of life with other people. In retrospect I understood more about the gift of spontaneous meditation, which—in any moment—can shift the part of me that resists peace. Peace does not coexist with doubt and worry. The sacred is everywhere, in everything, in everyone.

Though the ideas of acceptance and change may seem mutually exclusive, in reality the interplay of the two ideas points to the important sacred principles that come up over and over again: being with what is; letting everything be as it is; and letting everyone be as they are. This resonates with the way we clear away the negative fog of thinking and belief, accepting and then replacing thoughts and beliefs with truth. The theme of acceptance and change is prominent in the simple practice of mindfulness meditation, too, where the mind is focused and alert, accepting whatever thought or emotion arises, and allowing it to pass on its own without fighting it or feeding it, then coming back to a centering focus.

Change and acceptance are defining aspects of being in space and time, and so acceptance and change rule the later years. Some say that, in the second half of life more than at any other time, new beginnings are critical to our physical, mental, and spiritual well-being. This is true in part because you're swimming upstream in a river of longstanding, stereotypical belief about aging. Society's dominant view is that loss and decline are the most significant things about this time of life: that slowly and inevitably we are losing our mind, our body, our spirit. That somehow vitality, engagement, and passion are available in the later years only to a few lucky people. But consider again moments of truth that come through grace when you are deeply absorbed in discovery or sharing some aspect of your deep expression.

In 2008, the World Science Festival held a session on longevity called "90 Is the New 50." If you're going to spend a hundred years on the planet, what will it be about? In some cultures, people of a certain age are considered elders, and elders are regarded as venerable teachers, respected for their wisdom. Whether or not ours is one of those cultures, there is a new horizon, where the older teacher becomes the young student, the wage-earning woman in the second half of life becomes the volunteer, the artist becomes the scientist, and the athlete becomes the trainer. Embracing age means letting go of stereotypes, letting the years count for gains made, and allowing the past to be prologue or nothing.

Although I was still teaching and writing, the new direction held a good deal of energy. One night, I had a dream that spoke to me about the direction I was choosing.

In the dream my grandmother—my mother's mother—is center stage. She has that familiar gray streak in her hair, and the row of tight curls at the back of her neck. We are in a large room somewhere with other people, and she is walking among them, as if she's the hostess of a fabulous gathering. She is wearing a swanky ensemble—a three-piece, crepe, maroon-colored affair with an outer coat, short jacket, and skirt. She seems pleased to be wearing something so beautiful: she swings the coat open and lets her hands fall casually on her hips. In the dream, I am wowed by my grandmother, so comfortable in her own skin. She has style and confidence. I see her as courageous. In the dream, I cross the floor to her side of the room, and indicate to the rest of the assembled group that I am in her entourage, related to her, choosing to be like her. I say to the rest of the assembled group, "I'm going with her."

When I awakened, I weighed the fact that I had never had a close emotional tie with my grandmother. My relationship with her had always been mediated by my mother, and I had never considered a direct connection. When I was a girl, she worked as a cleaning lady for families in one of the wealthiest counties in the Midwest. Once or twice a year, she would bring bags of gently used clothing for whichever one of us could wear them— expensive castoffs that had once belonged to Mary and Marie Webster. Their name labels were sewn into all of their clothes, and I assumed that they were twins. Most of their dresses fit me with little or no altering.

At the time my grandmother had made her transition, I had long since been a mother making my own way, but not yet a writer. In my memories of her, she was never sick. Though she died of congestive heart failure, in my view, a worn-out heart was not the same as an illness.

Awake after the dream, I remembered stories about her women's-club meetings, the delicious foods they served, the lovely appointments. I remembered winks and nods about her men friends. The foundations of the spiritual temple where she was held in high regard strayed far from traditional religion. In her eighties, she was the director of social activities in the senior citizens' building where she lived. I remembered hearing a description of her wearing a floor-length gray satin gown to one of their affairs.

I interpreted my dream as the out-picturing of me coming into awareness of choosing to identify with my vital self, engaged with living. In the second half of life, there is always the possibility of new beginnings. Acceptance of what we cannot change and willingness to change what we can fosters the wisdom to know the difference. There is no such thing as too late, or already done. You are always coming into your next best-yet-to-be, waking up again and again to your newest expression.

In a tribute to Steve Jobs, his sister, the writer Mona Simpson, said that his final six syllables were, "OH WOW. OH WOW. OH WOW." No one can know what he meant, but I like to think that this artistic entrepreneur and titan of technological innovation was on the bridge between an ending and a new beginning. Again.

Your crucial next step—identifying the next expression that is yours to consciously embody—can be like stepping off a cliff. It is the beginning of a new beginning, with no assurances about where you will land. But you have a parachute. You have the net of conviction that you are a child of the universe, no less than the trees and the stars; you have a birthright to be at this place and time. What you seek is already yours.

Cultivating the Practice of Contemplation

What you believe about yourself and your connection to all that is has everything to do with the aim of contemplation. In this practice, you look at what you can accept as yours to be, do, or have, whether it is a sacred truth or a creative expression. Usually you associate it with long and thoughtful observation. Focusing your thinking about personal expression, personal development, and spiritual growth is essential to anyone interested in expansion. Actual study—no matter how old you are—can be an adjunct to this kind of careful and lengthy consideration.

What is true attracts us, in the way we are attracted to remembered things. Truth can disturb the waters again and again. A new passion attracts us much in the same way. If you come across an idea to which you are already in opposition, an attraction to this "outlier" can muddy things. You hear something contradictory, and you begin to gather evidence to corroborate your long-held view. If you're in doubt, you question whether it is a new concept or the same thing in new clothing. And then you choose to be open or to resist.

Through contemplation, you open to new possibilities altogether. No matter your perspective, what is true is true, and on some level, it is possible to apprehend it. You seek and inevitably you encounter something spoken, read, or otherwise perceived, and you conclude: this is for me. When information is coupled with belief, a certain perspective, and sound judgment, it becomes knowledge. You believe that you have uncovered a new idea that you can accept.

Hearing your truth does not necessarily translate into knowing your truth on a spiritual or human level. Pete Wilson, author of the bestselling book *Plan B: What Do You Do When God Doesn't Show Up the Way You Thought He Would?*, explores this idea in a blog post titled "Information Does Not Equate To Transformation." You must ponder, come at it from different angles. To have a revelation or a realization is to have an experience, a demonstration, a confirmation. The truth that you experience is the circumstance that can give rise to your transformative shift into deep recognition.

Having that experience can mean stepping outside comfortable boundaries, risking whatever you must in order to find out. Sometimes you fly without a net, try on principles that are both threatening and appealing. But when you turn your head in the direction of your desire to do, be, have, or know, you indicate that you are open to receive everything you need in order to embrace whatever comes to you.

In *The Shoes of the Fisherman*, Morris West says, "It costs so much to be a full human being, that there are few of us who have the courage or the enlightenment to pay the cost.… One must court doubt and darkness as the cost of knowing."

As with other spiritual practices, the aim of contemplation is to step out on our conviction in our ordinary living as well as in our sacred moments, and act on that knowing.

Contemplation Exercises

1. Consider using your journal as you respond to this prompt: Recall the most recent time that you came to know something that, rationally, you could not have known. Recall your response to that experience, and whether or not you shared it with anyone.

2. Sit with these questions and write out your responses to the questions as well as any insights that come: Is there something else in life that you are supposed to be doing or being, and you don't know what that is? Or is there something you want to do, and you know what it is, but you can't seem to get

started? Is there something that you love doing, and you have kept it a secret, doing it periodically as your personal reward for finishing your "real" work? Are you in a holding pattern?

Additional Exercises

1. In a more general way over time, trust the process. Get outside of your usual mode of taking in knowledge or observing the world that you have taken for granted. For example: Be a kid again. Go to a planetarium. Find a fossil. Watch an ant colony. See a white tiger. Lie on your back on a dark night and observe the starry sky. Take in the essence of a wildflower. Visit a place where minds unlike yours commune in a life-affirming manner. Record your insights.

2. From your journal, find any entry related to your ponderings about an often ignored or taken-for-granted creative aspect of yourself. How might that be out-picturing in your life?

AFTERWORD

There is a word among infinite verses in the eternal poem of the universe. That word is ours to utter. In the narrative of our own uniqueness, it is the highest utterance, completing the line, satisfying the crescendo of that part of the poem. That word in that timing is a fulfillment. To allow your word to go unspoken is to shut down the energy of crescendo in your life, and resist the upward pull of our purpose. The poem runs inside each of us; we hear it individually. No one else knows whether or not you are speaking your word, but you do.

SOURCES

Page 26: David Hawkins, *Power vs. Force: The Hidden Determinants of Human Behavior* (Hay House, 1995), 238.

Page 38: William C. Bridges, *Transitions: Making Sense of Life's Changes* 2nd ed. (Perseus Books Group, 2004), xii.

Page 45: Coleman Barks, trans., *The Essential Rumi, New Expanded Edition*, (HarperOne, 2004), 36.

Page 58: Holy Bible, ASV, Romans 12:2.

Page 59: Sri Aurobindo, Kena Upanishad text and translation, www.aurobindo.ru/workings/sa/12/kena_e.pdf.

Page 59: James Baquet, "Aldous Huxley and the Perennial Philosophy: An Introduction to the Basic Concepts," dalkeyarchive.com.

Pages 64: Rick Hanson, PhD with Richard Mendius, MD, *Buddha's Brain: The Practical Neuroscience of Happiness, Love, and Wisdom* (New Harbinger Publications, Inc., 2009), 85-86.

Pages 84: Dave Weich, "Annie Leibovitz at Work," Powell'sBooks. Blog, November 30, 2008, www.powells.com/blog/interviews/annie-leibovitz-at-work-2-by-dave/.

Page 86: Michael Bernard Beckwith, *Life Visioning*, Sounds True Audio Learning Course, produced by Paul Hoffman of Agape Media International (Sounds True, 2008).

Page 86: Janet Bray Attwood and Chris Attwood, T*he Passion Test: The Effortless Path to Discovering Your Life Purpose* (Plume, 2006), xvii.

Page 98: Barks, *The Essential Rumi, New Expanded Edition*, 36.

Page 119: Michael Bernard Beckwith, foreword to *Frequency: The Power of Personal Vibration* by Penney Peirce (Atria Books/Beyond Words, 2009).

Page 124: George Bartzokis, M.D., in *The Talent Code: Greatness Isn't Born. It's Grown. Here's How* by Daniel Coyle, (Arrow Books, 2010), 6

Pages 165–166: Cami Walker, *29 Gifts: How a Month of Giving Can Change Your Life* (Da Capo Lifelong Books, 2009).

Page 183: Barks, *The Essential Rumi, New Expanded Edition*, 109.

Page 188: Mona Simpson, "A Sister's Eulogy for Steve Jobs," *The New York Times,* October 30, 2011, www.nytimes.com/2011/10/30/opinion/mona-simpsons-eulogy-for-steve-jobs.html?pagewanted=all&_r=0.

Page 189: Pete Wilson, "Information Does Not Equate to Transformation" (blog entry), www.withoutwax.tv/2009/11/30/information-does-not-equate-to-transformation/.

Page 190: Morris West, *The Shoes of the Fisherman* (The Vatican Trilogy), Kindle edition (The Toby Press, 2013).

IN GRATITUDE

I am grateful for the Infinite Giving-ness that is ever pouring forth as my life. It would be impossible to thank each person who has brought some treasure—tangible or intangible—to the manifestation of this book, but I do. I thank my sister-friends Bettye Wages and Sandra Carpenter for decades of loving, brilliant, and ridiculous truth-telling marathons, and weathering the waves together. I am grateful for innumerable teachers who have set guideposts along the way; for William Fabian who shed light on the shadowy parts. I am grateful to the Light Ladies group for our outings, feasts, and celebrations that keep it Light, and to everyone at Celebration Center and everyone who has ever been there for knowledge, inspiration, and the experience of community. I thank Jody Bolz, a gifted poet, smart reader, consummate editor, and friend, whose superb insight urged me toward the best narrative stance for the book. I thank Rosalyn Story, a phenomenal writer and intuitive friend who—in the face of my shelving the rough draft—sent an email to Doug. I am grateful to Doug Seibold, my publisher, for seeing something worth saying and taking a chance that others will see it too; to Rachel Hinton, my editor at Agate, for her painstaking gift of ensuring that what gets said makes meaning without too many clichés or too few examples, and keeps the best words in the best order; and for everyone at Agate for the amazing feat of turning Times New Roman on all-purpose paper into something lovely to hold and behold.

ABOUT THE AUTHOR

Maxine Clair grew up in Kansas City, Kansas. She earned a Bachelor of Science degree at the University of Kansas and worked for nearly two decades as a medical technologist at Children's National Medical Center in Washington, DC. As she approached midlife and experienced the disquiet that comes with inner redefinition, she earned an MFA in creative writing at American University. In this new career she became a successful poet, fiction writer, and professor of English at George Washington University in Washington, DC. Her books include the poetry collection *Coping With Gravity,* the award-winning collection of interconnected stories *Rattlebone,* and the novel *October Suite.*

In 2009, her desire to share the experience of continual awakening to greater possibilities led her to pursue a license to coach others through Centers for Spiritual Living. In addition to private coaching, teaching classes, and conducting workshops, she facilitates weekly meditation in Falls Church, Virginia.

Q. & A. WITH MAXINE CLAIR

Your books always drew from the well of autobiography, to some degree, but *Imagine This* is the first that contains overtly autobiographical sections. Did you ever imagine you would write this?

My life and how I have experienced it is what I know. Memory and imagination are very closely aligned whether I'm writing actual fact or fiction. That familiar ground informs my writing process and the content. In my character-driven stories, the characters, events, and situations are invented. But their emotional and psychological responses to life come through the filter of what I know: as a maker, how aware I am of realistic possibilities. Stories flow from that. Universality flows from that combination. I am always pursuing expansiveness for my characters, whether we call it "coming of age" or "coming to terms with life." Inner conflict gives rise to outer conflict, and resolution follows the same inner-outer pattern. At some point, I wanted to go beyond the mental or psychological inner conflicts and explore metaphysical principles as the deeper cause and effect. The nonfiction form seemed to be the best fit, and so I chose it for *Imagine This*. In writing the book, I got to play just as deeply in language as I do in fiction. Though memoir can get dicey when I tease out what is and is not relevant to the work at hand, autobiography offers no such choice. For me, that's the good news. Autobiography is necessarily a voluminous venture. I never imagined that I would not write memoir. And I never imagined that I would not find a way to include the metaphysical.

Did you find the shift from fiction to nonfiction difficult? Has it affected your prose or identity as a writer?

There was a clear hiatus in my writing, a time when I wondered if I would ever write another conflict-resolution story. With *Imagine This*, the difficulty in navigating the shift to nonfiction had more to do with sustaining coherence between the narrative slices of memoir and exposition that includes how-to exercises and examples. I did not consciously adopt other stylistic elements; my voice is my voice and I trust that that will always come through in the prose. Usually there is a moral imperative, and I must find a way to tease it out. I was aware of reining in my imagination when it wanted to take over the narrative. There seems to be a little more leeway for poetic elements to creep in as I write stories. Yet, in writing *Imagine This*, I found a sufficient degree of "poetic" freedom—it is hoped—to ward off any persistent infection of flat prose.

As far as identity is concerned, I am a writer. The marriage of content and form is a foundational notion to which I subscribe. The form is determined by what I wish to convey. These days, as long as the work is interesting, few readers outside the academy care what genre terms we use, or how we mix the elements. Critics, too, are probably willing to stretch definitions and hyphenate labels.

Who are your influences, in writing and life, and how have they made their presence felt in *Imagine This*?

I never like this question, because I don't believe I can know all of the influences. Much of what influences us is unconscious. I am born into a certain place and time, and ideas and ways of expressing them can be pervasive throughout my sphere of living. But I will say what I have said many times, music is at the root of my love for language, and putting that together with any moral imperative, any idea that begs exploration can be put down in one form or another. Allowing that flow is my love for writing.

My mother's creatively expressive music was my greatest conscious influence. Her gospel cadences shot through with jazz are still like cell memory, and that can never be lost. Improvisation finds its own way in language—consider the cross-over of scat-bob and rap. It found its way into my own voice. So maybe it's in the DNA. When I encountered the women writers of the Black Arts Movement, like Toni, Alice, Lucille, N'tozake, Maya, June, Sonia, Nikki—I purposely omit surnames to illustrate the iconic stature of these women—there was a clear resonance. Rather than "influence," I believe I took permission from them. Yes, I stand on their shoulders, but at the time, they conveyed to me that it was entirely correct and life-affirming to make art of whatever you want to say in your own unique way, and let the power of it stand on its own merits. They expanded the canon for me when my vision of a canon was limited. Lo and behold, my voice was what having a "literary canon" was all about.

Did you find it difficult to wrestle concepts like creativity into practical, reproducible terms?

"Challenging" is a more accurate term for this undertaking. I was compelled to return again and again to my own simple, fundamental definition of creativity: bringing a no-thing into existence as something. Obviously this makes open-ended any discussion of the concept of creativity. It provides a platform from which I could marry the idea of creative expression as a portal to personal transformation, and some of the principles involved in manifesting anything in life. And since I could never put a dent in the volume of writings about such sweeping concepts, I could share my own experience of this avenue to transformation, which I see as a sacred journey. I believe that if *Imagine This* resonates with readers at all, it is because they are at a similar juncture in life. When you feel that there is more living inside of you than your life can contain, your life gets bigger. My conviction is that creative expression in any of limitless fields is a sure-thing avenue to a bigger life. I have spelled out ways of personal fulfillment and collective enrichment that come with such a venture.

Any final words of advice for struggling dream-seekers?

I want you to know that every life is uniquely remarkable. We can live making conscious choices about how we spend our time and energy or we can believe that life just happens to us. The choices you make about the work you would love to be doing are always tied to your life purpose, and will bring fulfillment. Finally, you create not what you want, but what you believe, and what you can accept. Wake up to wherever you are right now. Get clear about your passion. Keep going. The way to arrival and success is shorter now than it has ever been.

Also by Maxine Clair

EBOOK
ISBN: 978-1-57284-484-1

EBOOK
ISBN: 978-1-57284-483-4

PRAISE FOR *OCTOBER SUITE*

"A sweetly straightforward, lyrical style that builds a surprising amount of power as it moves quietly along.... Clair tells her story with a pitch-perfect feel for the time and the people."
—*Publishers Weekly*

PRAISE FOR *RATTLEBONE*

"Clair consistently attains the poetry organic to everyday speech.... [*Rattlebone* is] told in a style that is memorable for its ability to shift tones and to capture, in rich and controlled language, new levels of consciousness."
—*The Washington Post*

"Extraordinary.... Each skillful plot twist, each new wonderful character has the effect of a sip of literary love potion."
—*The New York Times Book Review*

AVAILABLE FOR PURCHASE WHEREVER EBOOKS ARE SOLD

AGATE
DIGITAL